On the West Highland Way

Jimmie Macgregor

Jimmie Macgregor is one of Britain's best-known folk-singers. His partnership with Robin Hall lasted more than twenty years, and in that time he made twenty-three long-playing records, and several singles and extended plays. Jimmie has long ago lost count of his radio and television performances, and he has appeared in all the country's great theatres and concert halls, as well as in colleges, universities, cathedrals, hotels, folk clubs, and town and village halls from the Channel Islands to the Shetlands.

He has taken his songs to Canada and the USA, Hong Kong, Israel, Austria, Australia and New Zealand, Hungary, Belgium, Holland, France, Germany, Russia, and the Middle East. Several of his own songs are used by fellow folk-singers, and he has produced records and composed and played theme music for radio and television. Since October 1982, he has presented his own highly successful daily radio show, *Macgregor's Gathering*, for BBC Radio Scotland.

Jimmie has worked as a hospital porter, engraver, school teacher, green-keeper, mortuary attendant, potter, quarryman, etc. He is a graduate of the Glasgow School of Art, and is a collector of pictures, glass, ceramics, old cars, furniture, and a wide variety of junk. His other obsessions are the outdoors, ornithology, and anything and everything Scottish.

D1102828

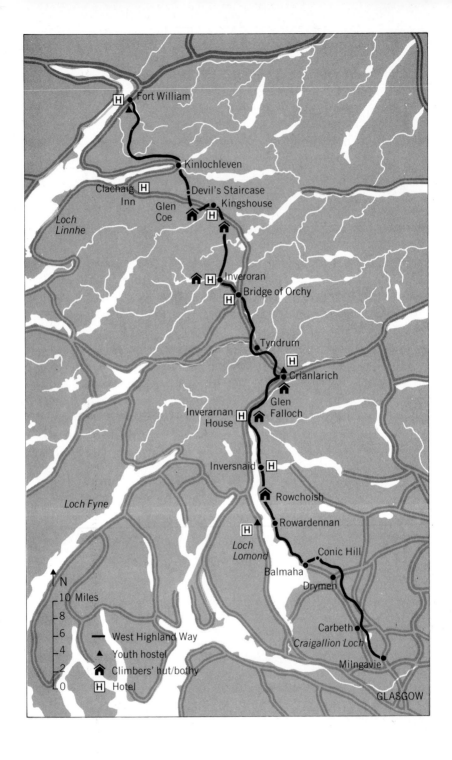

Fort William

H

Kinlochleven

Clachaig
Inn   H   Devil's Staircase
Glen   Kingshouse
Coe   H   H

Loch
Linnhe   Inveroran
                                      H   Bridge of Orchy
                                            H

                                                  Tyndrum

                                            H   Crianlarich

                                                  Glen
Inverarnan   Falloch
House   H

                                            Inversnaid   H

                                                  Rowchoish
Loch Fyne
                                                  Rowardennan

                              Loch
                              Lomond   Conic Hill
                                            Balmaha
                                                  Drymen

                                            Carbeth
                    N   Craigallion Loch
          10 Miles
          8   Milngavie
          6
          4   West Highland Way
          2   ▲   Youth hostel
          0   🏠   Climbers' hut/bothy
                   H   Hotel
                                                  GLASGOW

on the

West Highland Way

Jimmie Macgregor

with photographs by the author

BRITISH BROADCASTING CORPORATION

By the same author:

Jimmie Macgregor's Folk-songs of Scotland (Volumes I and II)
Singing our Own
Scottish and Border Battle Ballads (with Michael Brander)
Macgregor's Gathering of Scottish Dialect Poetry

The map of the West Highland Way is reproduced by courtesy of
the Countryside Commission for Scotland

Published by the
British Broadcasting Corporation
35 Marylebone High Street
London W1M 4AA

ISBN 0 563 20125 8

First published 1985
© Jimmie Macgregor 1985

Filmset by August Filmsetting, St. Helens.
Printed in England by
R.J. Acford Ltd
Chichester, Sussex

Contents

How it Was

On the West Highland Way I was alternately exhilarated and exhausted. I briskly breezed along on open hillsides, and I doggedly slogged on bouldery braes. In some places there was fine progress on the springy turf covering old tracks and disused railway lines, and in others I dragged my sodden boots through clinging glutinous glaur*. I was mutilated by midges and clobbered by clegs*. Sometimes sunburned, sometimes soaked, I was weary, windblown and weatherbeaten. The second day, however, was less eventful.

* *glaur*: mud * *clegs*: horse flies
NB There may be a few more words like this in the book. I'll explain as I go along.

People who Helped

Any serious attempt to acknowledge all the people who helped to set me on the West Highland Way would involve going back to my boyhood, and an old Scoutmaster called Ian Mackie, who was one of the first people to introduce me to the outdoors, and who gave me my first interest in wildlife. I am grateful to him, and to everyone who ever told me a tale, or passed on a little of their knowledge. Like the person who first suggested that a twig thrown in a billycan of boiling tea would absorb the taste of smoke from a campfire. (It doesn't work, but I've always done it. A bit daft really, because, in fact, I *like* smoky tea.) I am indebted too, to the botanist who told me of the little ivy-leaved toadflax which, when the time comes to reproduce itself, turns its tiny flower completely around and shoots its seeds back into the lime-rich mortar of the old walls on which it thrives. How can I repay the gamekeeper who, long ago, walked me, at his own murderous pace, across a moor on the Island of Lewis, to a cliff where I had my first unforgettable sighting of a golden eagle in the wild? These people, and many others, opened my eyes and ears to all the things I was to enjoy on the West Highland Way. This list of acknowledgements must of necessity be incomplete, and if I omit anyone, it is simply because a comprehensive catalogue would occupy the whole of this book. However, among those I must thank are Christopher Irwin and Richard Titchen of Radio Scotland, for endorsing my idea for the radio series on which the book is based; Ben Lyons, my producer, for his enormous skill and patience in editing the mass of tapes which I brought back from my walk and Malcolm Payne, Public Relations Officer for the Countryside Commission for Scotland, for a very informative interview, and a great deal of advice and assistance. Many people contributed to my enjoyment of the walk; and to all of them – the foresters, naturalists, anglers, mountaineers, and to fellow walkers met along the way, (especially the four Dutch girls and the two Derbyshire lads who had a special appreciation of the route,) – I say again, 'Thank you'.

Opposite The author, Loch Lomond and the Ben

About the Way

The West Highland Way is Scotland's first official long-distance footpath. It was declared open in October 1980, and I walked it in late May/early June 1981. By the end of that first season, the way had been well publicised, and was attracting even more walkers than had been anticipated. The numbers have continued to increase, and the West Highland Way is now being enjoyed by people from all over Britain and from other countries. They are of all ages, and range from complete beginners to seasoned hardy types with experience of other long-distance paths. Outdoor people in the west of Scotland are already familiar with most of the ground traversed by the Way, and I explored it in my teens and student days, though never as a continuous route.

The Countryside Commission for Scotland must be given great credit for the overall organisation of the way, and for overcoming endless problems in establishing it, but the first glimmerings of the idea appeared away back in the twenties and thirties. It was during

Way-marker, Milngavie

the last Depression that people from the great industrial sprawl of Glasgow and its environs had time on their hands, and discovered the wilderness almost on their doorsteps. Cycling, hill-walking and climbing clubs were formed, some of them now very famous, and organised routes began to be discussed. It was in 1969 however, that a very dedicated and able man called Tom Hunter skilfully co-ordinated the expertise and enthusiasm of the Glasgow group of the Holiday Fellowship with other outdoor clubs, in the first proper survey of a potential route. It is a tribute to the skill of Tom Hunter and his colleagues that after more than ten years of problems with access, rights of way, farmers, landowners and so on, the West Highland Way follows almost exactly the route which was originally proposed.

The walk can be taken in either direction, but I suggest that it be followed from south to north. The route is attractive and interesting from the first step, but there is no doubt that the prospect widens and the landscapes grow grander and more dramatic as one advances into the Highlands, climaxing with the high remoteness of the Lairig Mhor, and the approach to the great lowering massif of Ben Nevis. The route also becomes more demanding in the northerly reaches, and for an inexperienced, or not fully-fit walker, the gradually increasing rigors will allow a build-up of strength.

My own reasons for walking the West Highland Way were firstly, sheer self-indulgence and, secondly, to collect material for a series of programmes on the walk for BBC Radio Scotland, so a portable tape recorder had to be added to my basic equipment. I shall talk briefly about outdoor gear later on, but at this point I should like to recommend two items which will add tremendously to your under-standing and enjoyment of the Way. The first is Tom Hunter's book *A Guide to the West Highland Way*. The book was published before the route was opened, and there have been some minor changes since it appeared, but it is crammed with fascinating information on wildlife, history, land use, forestry, conservation, and many other aspects of the country which the route explores. You should also have the Countryside Commission for Scotland's official guide by Robert Aitken, together with the map of the route. These items should be in every walker's pack. They are not meant simply to be read, however, but to get you out there to experience it all for yourself. My own book will be a very personal impression of Scotland's first official long-distance footpath.

The Route

The West Highland Way is ninety-five miles (152 km) long, beginning at Milngavie, a few miles outside Glasgow, and ending at Fort William on Loch Linnhe. The Way follows the shore of Scotland's most famous loch, in the shadow of an equally famous mountain, crosses its widest and most desolate moor, and ends at the foot of its highest Ben. The walker will experience every kind of Scottish scenery, from gently pastoral to heavily wooded, and from the cheerful tourist havens to the silent lonely places. You'll scramble along tangled lochside paths, and plod your way across open moors. There are some uphill slogs, and wonderful wide open walks on the high passes. As the landscape changes, so does the plant, animal and bird life, and for the naturalist, the whole walk is a rich delight. You will follow ancient rights of way, old railway lines, forestry paths, the military roads of Wade and Caulfield, and walk in the footsteps of the old Scottish drovers. The main sections of the route are:

Milngavie — Carbeth. *Four and one-quarter miles (7 km).*

Carbeth — Drymen. *Seven and three-quarter miles (12.5 km).*

Drymen — Balmaha. *Six and one-half miles (10.5 km).*

Balmaha — Rowardennan. *Seven and one-quarter miles (11.75 km).*

Rowardennan — Inversnaid. *Seven and one-quarter miles (11.75 km).*

Inversnaid — Invernan. *Six and one-half miles (10.5 km).*

Invernan — Crianlarich. *Six and one-half miles (10.5 km).*

Crianlarich — Tyndrum. *Six and one-half miles (10.5 km).*

Tyndrum — Bridge of Orchy. *Six and three-quarter miles (10.75 km).*

Bridge of Orchy — Inveroran. *Two and one-half miles (4.00 km).*

Inveroran — Kingshouse. *Nine and one-half miles (15.25).*

Kingshouse — Kinlochleven. *Nine miles (14.5 km).*

Kinlochleven — Lundavra. *Seven and one-half miles (12.00 km).*

Lundavra — Fort William. *Six and one-half miles (10.5 km).*

It is quite obvious that the walk can be undertaken in short, moderate, or long stages, and is thus accessible to the casual ambler, at least in the southern sections, as well as to the hardened hill-walker. There are also people who would never dream of attempting the whole route, who are able to enjoy various stretches. However, I do strongly recommend that the Way should be treated as an entity, as its real beauty is in the constantly changing scene, and developing wildness. I understand the tiger who gets his head down and knocks the whole thing off before lunch, so that he can jog up Ben Nevis in the afternoon, but he misses a great deal by not being able to stop and stare.

The start, Milngavie

Looking After the Countryside

The outdoor people I knew in my youth were fanatical about preserving the countryside, and this long before words like conservation and ecology fell out of the lexicon and into everyday conversation. After breaking camp, the area would be scoured as a matter of routine, and litter would be burned or taken way. Tin cans were flattened and buried, and campfires thoroughly doused with water, then covered with earth or sand. The idea was that if anyone happened on your campsite half an hour after you had left, they should not know that you had ever been there. The principle is still a good one, for litter is now pollution, and has become a serious problem. Not so very long ago, the countryside would quickly absorb anything abandoned or missed by the few people who were out and about, but now, with the growing numbers of people enjoying the outdoors, the dangers are greatly increased. If each person walking the West Highland Way were to leave behind one wrapper or container, we should soon be up to the oxters* in garbage, and the problem is exacerbated by the fact that so much modern wrapping is of material which resists natural decay, or is, to use the current jargon, non biodegradable. Some of these materials will resist the elements almost indefinitely, and any which contain traces of food, or even salt, can be a deadly trap for wildlife. Fish are killed in some numbers by swallowing plastic cartons, and even animals as large as deer sometimes do not survive eating plastic bags.

It may not always be obvious that the countryside which is your pleasure is also someone else's place of work, but you should remember that even something as simple as an unclosed gate can cause havoc among livestock and crops. If you have to climb a gate, a fence or a dyke, take care. They are there for a reason, and the average townie would be horrified at how much they cost. My own attitude to dogs on the West Highland Way is that they simply shouldn't be there, but if you must take your pet, keep it under strictest control. A dog doesn't actually have to attack an animal to cause damage. It can stampede cattle or terrify a pregnant ewe into aborting. One would hope that the kind of people who take to the Way would not think of picking wild flowers, a pastime which is, of

* *oxters*: armpits

course, illegal, and it should be obvious that branches broken from living trees don't burn as well as the dead ones which are lying around. Fires should really be avoided however, as they are a tremendous hazard, even on open moorland, as well as in wooded areas. A sure sign of the tyro camper is the huge fire which creates clouds of smoke, blackens all the utensils, and turns handles red hot. A tiny fire no bigger than your fist, if placed between a few stones tunnelled to the wind, is much more efficient, but it's better, and much safer, to use a stove. If you observe these little rules, avoid pollution of streams, lochs and rivers, and don't go wandering off across private land, the Way-walkers will remain welcome. People who live and work along the route will be found to be friendly and helpful in the main, but avoid pestering them. A friend, John Groome, was more amused than annoyed by the scores of people who came to his door for a kettle of water. John lived a few yards from millions of gallons of the purest water in Britain: Loch Lomond.

Looking After Yourself

Accommodation on the West Highland Way is fairly plentiful and quite varied, but without doubt, a tent offers the greatest freedom. Camping obviates the need to find and book a place to sleep, and it has great advantages in allowing a flexible schedule, and keeping one in contact with the outdoor environment. There are, however, certain stretches of the Way where camping is discouraged. These areas are the Balmaha side of Conic Hill, from Inversnaid to Crianlarich, and the short stretch between Tyndrum and Bridge of Orchy. Camping equipment also adds considerably to the load which has to be carried, and there is a great deal to be said for travelling light. There are some hotels on most parts of the route but the ones which cater specially for Way-walkers are the Inversnaid Hotel on Loch Lomond, Inverarnan House Hotel, to the north and on the other side of the Loch, the Bridge of Orchy Hotel on the Glencoe road, and the old Inveroran Hotel at Loch Tulla. Other hotels can be found in the Scottish Tourist Board's book, *Where to Stay in Scotland*. Private bed and breakfast accommodation can be found along the whole route, and there are four Youth Hostels: Rowardennan, Crianlarich, Glencoe and Glen Nevis. The most interesting sleeping place I used was the Rowchoish bothy on Loch Lomond side. This was built as a memorial to one of the early Scottish outdoor men, William Ferris, and is pretty basic. One of the walls is only half height, so that side is open to the elements, but there is a fireplace, plenty of wood, and a good roof. Two things to remember are first, that there is considerable pressure on accommodation in the West Highlands in the high season, and secondly, that there are stretches where there is nothing, and once you start off, you must continue. Keep an eye on your map, but these stages are, notably, between Inveroran and Kingshouse, and the long haul from Kinlochleven to Fort William. Take note also of the best places to stock up on provisions.

For any but the hardiest and most experienced of walkers, to attempt the Way in winter would be foolhardy, and positively dangerous. Even in the early spring and late autumn, it has to be remembered that the days are short, and early starts are essential to avoid being caught by darkness. Don't undertake the walk if you feel that you are not reasonably fit. You will only feel miserable, and slow down any companions. Three or four weeks of brisk daily walks of a few miles should be all that is required to start you off, and your fitness will sharpen up quite quickly once you are under way.

Care of the feet is absolutely crucial, for even if you have the physique of King Kong and the determination of Margaret Thatcher, or vice versa, broken blisters will bring you to a miserable halt. At Inveroran, by an incredible stroke of good fortune, I met a professional chiropodist. Tom (Toes) Taggart was walking the Way with his family, and he suggested that every walker should carry a basic foot kit, consisting of powder, plaster in rolls of various widths, (the small individual plasters tend to rub off rather quickly), some cotton wool and chiropody felt for cushioning blisters, and most importantly, a small pair of scissors for cutting all this stuff. With the proper socks and footwear, the problem should never arise, but I have discovered from experience that instant attention to any discomfort can save a lot of trouble. Don't decide to do another few miles; you'll have a blister by then. Stop immediately, and attend to the sensitive spot. As my boots were not quite so well broken in as I'd have liked, I applied a double thickness of plaster to my heels before I took a step, and I'm sure that it protected me from damage. There was a reason for my starting the walk in almost new boots, but as a basic principle, your footwear should be well broken in before you take on a walk like the West Highland Way.

What You'll Need

My training for the West Highland Way consisted of hammering round Highgate Woods in north London every day for several weeks. Rain or shine, I wore several sweaters, an anorak, and my old hill boots, which had got to the stage where they fitted my feet like a second skin. There was a mere shadow of tread on the soles, but I calculated that they were good for another few hundred miles. Ten days before I was due to start the walk, both boots hinted that they had perhaps done enough, by splitting straight across the soles. This tragedy forced me to revue all my gear, and the conclusions were depressing. There was a vintage Bergen rucksack, and a two-man tent which weighed about the same as a three-room bungalow. The poles were collapsible oak trees with solid brass couplings. I had a sinister-looking dark-green, oily ground-sheet which, when cold, could only be unfolded by a man with seventeen-inch biceps. So, off I went to Nevisport in Glasgow, where Bryan Chambers suggested that my equipment might be of some interest if Nevisport ever established an outdoor museum. He then supplied me with a superb pair of boots which, with frequent applications of neat's-foot oil and constant wear, were reasonably flexible when I took off from Milngavie. I was shown a two-man tent which weighed less than my boots, but which was guaranteed to withstand sub-zero temperatures. The collapsible frame was of fibreglass sections, slim as reeds. Very expensive, and a trifle exotic for the West Highland Way, but there were quite inexpensive tents which were ideal for the job. A flysheet, by the way, is not a luxury, but an essential in bad weather, and it can often be pitched first, and the tent itself then erected under its protection. Don't, whatever you do, buy your tent from one of those general hardware stores, as you are likely to be sold a backyard toy. Any good outdoor shop will advise you. Tell them what your needs are, and they will supply the appropriate equipment. Most of the assistants in these shops are experienced outdoor people, and take a pride in their knowledge of their equipment.

You will meet people, as I did, on the Way, wearing training shoes, wellies, even street shoes, and perhaps they'll get away with it, but they would be in real trouble in bad weather, or if they have the misfortune to turn an ankle. Boots are essential. Make sure you get the right ones for the job, and buy the best you can afford. The correct socks are important too, and again, it pays to take advice. You'll need a fine inner pair, as well as the heavier outer ones, and don't forget some spares. Gaiters are very useful in the wet, especially when walking through high vegetation, and you should have a pair of gloves and a woolly hat in your bag. (A very high proportion of body heat is lost through the head.) Torch, whistle, first aid kit, map and compass are standard equipment.

Choose your rucksack very carefully. It's crazy to buy a huge sack if you're only going to be doing short sections of the walk. Again, take advice. You may only require a 'lally bag', something big enough to carry a flask and a change of sweater and socks. If you're camping, you'll find that modern stoves and utensils are very light and compact. Plastic bags are another blessing for the modern camper. They make great waterproof linings for rucksacks, containers for spare clothes, and a big one can even go over your sleeping bag. Don't skimp on a sleeping bag, it's a very important item, but don't buy one designed for Everest if you're never going to go out in the winter. There have been vast improvements in recent years in outdoor clothing, and there are many good books on the subject. It always used to be said that you got wet on the hill, and that was that; for any outer garment which was dense enough to keep out the weather also caused perspiration and condensation. That problem has been tackled quite successfully, and there are now fabrics which are waterproof and which breathe as well. The basic idea in dressing for the outdoors remains the same, however. Several light layers of inner clothing are more effective than one heavy layer, and the outer 'shell' garments must keep out the wet, and be effective wind breakers. I tend to heat up very quickly, and it's really just as uncomfortable to be too hot as to be too cold, so I find that it's quite important that the shell clothing should easily ventilate at the neck, waist and wrists. Some of the better ones even have small zips in the armpits. A Youth Hostel membership card, and a pair of light binoculars are handy items.

Making a Start

"I hastened to prepare my pack, and tackle the steep ascent that lay before me . . ." That was Robert Louis Stevenson in *Travels with a Donkey in the Cevennes*. I hastened to prepare my pack and tackle the four-hundred-yard walk to Finnieston Station in Glasgow, where I would take the train to Milngavie, and the beginning of the West Highland Way. The most central point for these trains is Queen Street Station, and the journey is less than half an hour. It was early summer, and I arrived at Milngavie around nine o'clock in the morning. The day was mild, and there was a very light drizzle. I had arranged to interview a man called George McQuarrie, who was the south-west of Scotland organiser of the British Trust for Conservation Volunteers. George was waiting with a group of youngsters who were about to set off for Balmaha, which meant that they had about twenty cross-country miles before them. George told me that the BTCV had tackled most of the real donkey work on the footpath; projects such as bridge-building, clearing undergrowth, constructing stiles, tree-felling, and the bulk of the very important job of way-marking. I left George and his group awaiting a late arrival, made my way through the underpass, which bears an engraved map of the whole route, up the steps, and into the Milngavie shopping centre. This is where you should do any last-minute stocking up, for you will very quickly be out in open country.

Milngavie is attractive, with an air of being rather pleased with itself; and rightly so, for it is a clean and leafy place to live. It has always been a great stepping off point for the open spaces, and as a lad I used to travel out here by tramcar, to walk over the Stockiemuir to Carbeth and the Whangie. One of the great excitements of Milngavie in those days was the Bennie railplane which stood back off the road on its raised tracks, as one approached the tram terminus. The fantasies the railplane created in our minds of Flash Gordon and space travel, were only a little far-fetched, for George Bennie, its inventor, was far ahead of his time. He was born in 1892 and his railplane, which would have travelled at more than one hundred miles an hour, was accepted by the railway companies as a wholly viable proposition, but the Depression killed off its chances, and the rocket-shaped plane and its stretch of raised track were dismantled in 1956, a year before Bennie died. His idea is now used in several parts of the world.

Milngavie is pronounced Millguy, and there is a theory that the name comes from the Gaelic, *Muileann gaoithe*, a windmill, and there were indeed several mills in the village in times past. There was a theory that only the posh folk said 'Milngavie' and the rest of us said 'Millguy'. We used to have a rhyme which said:

When one's doing well, and one's deep in the gravy,
One lives in Millguy, but calls it Milngavie.

Another one, from the First World War, went:

Gin a body meet a cuddy*
Coming frae Mulguy,
Gin that cuddy's wet and muddy
Here's the reason why.
In Flanders muck a tank got stuck;
'Och weel,' says Jock Mackay,
I've seen the glaur a damn sicht waur*
When coming through Mulguy.

The West Highland Way leaves the town centre by a walkway over the stream, and in a few minutes I was in a leafy lane which used to be an old railway line, and rapidly leaving Milngavie behind. The light rain had left everything sparkling and fragrant, the sun was out, and I felt that I was really on my way. Insects were humming, and bird song was all around me. A gleaming cock blackbird with his brilliant orange bill rattled his alarm call up the lane, and the arrogant cadence of the chaffinch contrasted with the wistful song of a robin. A

* *cuddy*: horse, *waur*: worse.

cock bullfinch gave me a glimpse of his flashy breeding plumage, and I heard the first willow-warbler of the walk. That sweet sad song with its dying fall, was the one sound I was to hear from one end of the West Highland Way to the other. Only in the most remote and high places was it absent. I was already enjoying myself, and in a very short time I was making good progress along the Allander water, with the sun on my back, and the sound of the stream in my ears. After a short stretch on the bank, a way-marker takes you up to the right and on to the higher ground of the Allander park, a nice open airy walk with gorse, birch and broom all around. The birds here are yellowhammer and linnet, and already the ubiquitous meadow pipit. This is the wee bird which is known to many Scots as the heather lintie; but I've discovered that almost any small, brownish bird which country people can't identify, conveniently becomes a heather lintie, or moss cheeper.

Nice and Easy

The walking on the Allander park was a real pleasure, and it was equally agreeable through Mugdock wood. There is a well-defined track, which used to be the old carriageway to Craigallion House, and the wood itself was all sun-dappled shade; the silence accentuated, if anything, by the sounds of birds and insects. The place is a botanist's delight, with the common plants growing in profusion, and a few of the rarer ones to be found by those who know where to look. Among the more interesting is the butterwort, an odd little plant with the leaves gathered in a rosette close to the ground, and the dull purplish-blue flower raised on a frail stalk. The flower attracts insects in the normal way, and for the normal purposes, but the leaves have a different function. Any insect daft enough to alight on their surface, finds itself instantly trapped by a gummy liquid. Struggle only results in more of the liquid being produced, while the edges of the leaf begin to fold over. The leaf produces not only the viscous fluid which traps the victim but, from a separate set of glands, another liquid, similar to our own gastric juices, which digests and absorbs the unlucky beastie. Butterwort leaves used to be used by country people in the same way as rennet, to curdle milk, and Laplanders produced a kind of thick yoghurt by combining reindeer milk with them. Another plant which

Above Mugdock Wood *Below* Old Craigallion coach road

you'll see everywhere in Mugdock wood is the honeysuckle or woodbine. It is to be seen growing over old dead stumps and around the boles of the trees. The beautiful flower is almost without perfume, but come back at dusk, and the heavy fragrance is almost overpowering, for the honeysuckle seduces the nocturnal insects, especially the hawk-moth.

Mugdock wood has long associations with the distillation of illicit whisky, and has been the scene of a few punch-ups between the gaugers, or revenue men, and the lads who made the rare drop. Bearing in mind the outrageous duty the Scots have to pay on their own whisky, it's not at all surprising that some of my Glasgow friends have declared themselves more than happy to have a punch-up in the same cause, if only they could find someone to punch. The walk through the wood took me some considerable time, but only because I stopped to make some recordings, and having done that, stopped some more, just to stand and stare. It's a short step to the exit from the wood, however, where you'll turn left down a road for only a few yards, then right through a gate and on to another track running above and parallel to the Allander water. As I reached this point, the sky was brilliantly blue, with huge white clouds sailing very high. The hill on the other side of the Allander was brilliant with yellow broom, and the air was full of the strange, heavy perfume of hawthorn blossom. The track along to Craigallion was very muddy in places, and I was able to record some glorious sounds as my boots plowtered* through the glutinous muck. The scene rapidly opens out as you proceed along this track, and as well as the small birds, you begin to hear peewit, curlew, and redshank. I stopped in a clump of alder to record some of these, and a pair of long-tailed tits flew in, and started to feed a few yards from my hiding place; beautiful little creatures, in black, white, grey and pink.

After the mud, the walking becomes nice and easy, and the waters of Craigallion Loch soon come into view, with part of the Campsie hills, and the great dumpling-shaped bulk of Dumgoyne beyond. Dumgoyne is an extinct volcano, and the first real landmark on the Way.

* *plowtered*: work it out for yourself.   *Nice and Easy* 21

Early Outdoors

I stopped for coffee on a gentle slope facing Craigallion Loch, and I didn't choose the spot simply because it's beautiful, although it certainly is that. There is much more to this place than a pretty view. The loch was utterly calm that day; reeded on the near shore, and heavily wooded on the other. Coot, waterhen, and tufted duck were going about their business, and up on the hill, Craigallion House looked down grandly, in the snooty manner some of these big houses seem to have. Craigallion played a very important part in the early days of the outdoor movement in Scotland and, immediately across the water from where I sat, was the site of the famous Craigallion fire. This fire was lit by the unemployed who found their way here from Glasgow and the surrounding districts, during the last Depression. They came out, partly to attempt to live off the land, partly to ease the financial burden on their families, and partly to escape the crushing hopelessness and boredom of unemployment. They lived really rough; great friendships were formed, and for many, Craigallion was the start of the lifelong love of the outdoors. There were great sing-songs, and men signed on here to fight Fascism in the Spanish Civil War. The story now is that the Craigallion fire was never allowed to go out. I'd love to believe that, and maybe one day, I'll find out whether or not it's true, for there are still plenty of the old timers around who were there.

As I moved on from Craigallion towards Carbeth, memories came flooding back, for I had covered all of this ground as a boy. I was first brought out here by a very dedicated man called Ian Mackie. He was my Scoutmaster, and I have him to thank for introducing me to the outdoor life. I also have to thank the Boy Scouts for teaching me so many things which proved to be spectacularly useless in later life (and a few handy things, too).

The track from Craigallion runs into a plantation, and as I entered it, I found that a hare had somehow got itself in before me. The wood was fenced with a fine mesh, presumably against roe deer, and this poor hare was totally confused by the fact that it could go neither left nor right. It would sprint ahead, stop and have a think and, as my steady pace brought me nearer, would shoot off aimlessly once again. At last, it did an incredible body swerve, and shot past within a foot of me, to vanish in a tawny blur, back the way it had come.

Craigallion Loch and Dumgoyne

Carbeth is a place which has always been popular with outdoor people, and was a stopping place for the old Glasgow Wheelers and the climbers of the famous Craigdhu Club, not to mention generations of campers and hill-walkers. A feature of Carbeth, and another manifestation of the widespread enthusiasm for getting away from it all, is the number of wooden holiday huts in the area. A few can be seen from the footpath, but there are many, many more out of sight. Most of them were built just before, and just after the war, and they have obviously been very well cared for to last so long. There are so many layers of paint on most of them, that no one is quite sure whether or not there is still any wood underneath. As a lad, my idea of Shangri La was a wooden hut at Carbeth (*below*).

Open Spaces

Leaving Carbeth, you will follow a track which meets a road at a place called Balachalairy Yett*. After only a few hundred yards westward on this road, a way-marker directs you over a stile into Tinker's Loan. Tinker's Loan is a broad grassy ride, rising in a gentle slope between two dry stane dykes. As I negotiated the stile, a flash of russet caught my eye, and I immediately froze, one foot on the sward of the loan, and the other, rather awkwardly, still on the stile. The russet had vanished, but after a few seconds the tiny snake-like head and needly eyes of the weasel appeared from a hole half-way up the dyke. I watched, fascinated, as the whippy little beastie darted in and out of the holes and crannies of the wall, occasionally emerging into full view, and rearing up on its hindquarters to sniff the air. The animal completely ignored me, and seemed very agitated, but as a weasel always seems agitated, I though nothing of that, until the cause of the creature's unease suddenly appeared, in the form of a stoat. In spite of the difference in size, the weasel instantly attacked, and the two animals became a whirling ball of fur, darting and capering in a duel which was almost too fast for the eye to follow. They would break off now and then, disappearing into the wall in turns, only to re-emerge and pursue their screeching quarrel. After a while, they broke away, and vanished as suddenly as they had appeared, but as I made my way up the loan I could still hear them spitting and cursing in the runnels and cavities of the old stones. I couldn't guess at the cause of their scuffle, but I realised that I had just witnessed something that could cost a committed naturalist hours, days, or weeks of watching time.

The open spaces beyond the head of Tinker's Loan are the haunt of curlew, peewit, redshank and snipe, and a cautious and quiet approach to the crest of the rise can be rewarded by a sighting of some of these birds rising from their nest sites. The walker will wish to pause at the gate, as it's here that we have our first big open view on the West Highland Way. The ground drops away over open moor to the buildings of Arlehaven. On the left are the Kilpatrick hills and on the right, the Campsies, and ahead, beyond Arlehaven, the twin mounds of Dumgoyne and Dumgoyach; Dumgoyne smooth and green, Dumgoyach more conical and heavily wooded. The day was crisp and clear as I reached this point, and I found myself looking into the

* *yett*: gate

Above Dumgoyach and the Blane Valley from Tinker's Loan
Below Tinker's Loan

distant Highlands. The Crianlarich hills were clearly visible, and the grand bulk of Ben Lomond looked comfortingly close in the bright sunlight, but I was to find out that there was a fair bit of slogging to do before I was walking in its shadow.

There is some open, airy progress now, which takes you close by the cottages at Arlehaven, and even closer to the buildings of the farm at Dumgoyach. Walkers should be careful to cause as little disturbance as possible to the very tolerant occupants of these places. This stretch of moorland is quite wet here and there, and that is reflected in the plants of the area. All the common ones are there: bog myrtle, blaeberry, bog cotton, and so on, but in a very wet place, I came on a clump of exotic-looking flowers, which really looked like expensive escapees from a nursery. These were monkey-flowers, and they are indeed incomers. Brought from America about 1820, they seemed a most unlikely plant to find in the middle of a Scottish moor, with their large, flashy yellow flowers spotted with equally flashy red. The plant distributes its seeds by running water, and no doubt this is why it has been so successful in spreading all over the country.

As you approach the towering woods of Dumgoyach, you may see, above you on your right, the Dumgoyach standing stones. In the official guide, Robert Aitken dismisses these ancient monuments with a finely-turned phrase which I quoted in my radio series, and which I think will bear repetition here. He says: 'The stones have limited interest for close examination, and the walker can best contribute to their conservation by viewing them from a distance'.

Drams and Sangs, Pots and Dots

Let ither poets raise a fracas
Bout wines and vines and drunken Bachus;
And crabbit* names and stories rack us,
And grate oor lug.
I sing the juice Scotch bear* can mak us
In gless or jug.

The stretch from Tinker's Loan had been interesting, but fairly rough going, and I was quite looking forward to making up some time on the old Blane Valley Railway. This is reached by the lane behind Dumgoyach farm, which crosses an old wooden bridge over the Blane water. A few yards further on, to the left, is a big gate with a stile, which starts you off on the four miles or so of the old railway line. I started off on this with some enthusiasm, striding along, with cattle and sheep grazing in the flat fields on my left, and a wood full of bird-song on my right. I was no sooner into my stride, however, when I

* *crabbit*: ill-natured. *bear*: barley.

noticed something else on my right. Across the fields were the gleaming white buildings of the Glengoyne distillery, which has been producing fine malt whisky in the Blane valley for one hundred and fifty years or so. Well, it seemed downright churlish not to pay it a visit, so off I went. I was welcomed by a very affable fellow called Ian Birrell, who gave me an expert and very interesting dissertation on the whisky-making process. I made the tactical error, however, of asking for a definition of proofage, as applied to spirits, and in a couple of minutes my head was buzzing with temperatures, volumes of ethyl alcohol, distilled water, ignition points, and much other jargon which left me even more confused than I had begun. Ian told me quite a lot about illicit whisky-making in the old days, and pointed out that at one time it was simply looked on as a natural adjunct to farming. After the failure of the 1745 rebellion, the suppression of the Highlands and the opening of the country by Wade's and Caulfield's roads, the government officers and revenue men had much easier access to outlying areas, and the private distiller then had to be much more devious and resourceful to survive. Many of them were, and did, but illicit distilling, as a widespread activity, was on the way out. My talk with Ian Birrell gave me the idea of making a song for the radio programmes and I recorded it with fellow folk-singer, Alastair McDonald (*Hardy Drinking Lads* p.28).

Back on the Blane Valley Railway, I was soon making good time, sometimes walking on the way where the old track ran, and sometimes on top of the continuous mound which runs parallel to it on the left. This mound conceals a huge pipe which takes water from Loch Lomond, and distributes it all over central Scotland. After passing the Beech Tree Inn a few yards to my right (a very attractive place, by the way and obviously destined to become one of the regular watering holes on the route), I had to take briefly to the road once again, before re-joining the old railway track which takes you almost all the way to the village of Gartness. The old buildings of Killearn Hospital brought back some memories of singing to the patients there, with the Scottish folk-singer Josh McRae, who was later to play an important part in the folk-music revival. The bridge which crosses over to the tiny village of Gartness, is a superb vantage point for the 'Pots' where the salmon can be observed as they struggle up river to spawn, Gartness was the home of the philosopher and mathematician John Napier, whose family at one time owned the land around the village. Napier is world famous as the inventor of logarithms, but he

Hardy Drinking Lads

Come ye hardy drinking lads
And hae a dram wi' me;
We'll tak a drap o' the double strang
Where the gaugers cannae see.
CHORUS
So heist your glass, tak aff your dram,
Wi' Sandy, Jock and me;
We'll honour bold John Barleycorn,
And swack the baurley bree.

The gaugers they cam' up the burn,
And roon behind the hill;
They lookit intae the birkie wud,
And they found oor Sandy's still.
Chorus
They cowpt the mash intae the burn,
And stampit a' aroon;
They doused the fire and brak the worm,
And ca'd the kettle doon.
Chorus
But Sandy's ta'en his hazel stick,
And wi' mony a rant and roar;
He's gi'en the gaugers dunt for dunt,
And mebbe twa three more.
Chorus
The gaugers they hae ta'en the road,
Their heids and backs gey sair;
And Sandy says, 'We'll ca' awa,
And mak a drappie mair.'
Chorus
So come ye hardy drinking lads,
Wi' Sandy, Jock and me;
We'll gang tae the still at the back o' the hill,
And swack the baurley bree.
Chorus

© Jimmie Macgregor

gaugers: excise men. heist: raise. swack: swig. baurley bree: barley brew. birkie wud.: birch wood. cowpt: tipped. the worm: the copper coil. ca'd: pulled. gey sair: rather sore, or painful.

also devised a dot – the decimal point, which, in its time, probably had as dramatic effect as the invention of the computer.

The present bridge at Gartness was built in 1971, and replaces the beautiful old original, which had lasted from 1715. The old stone bearing that date has been built into the parapet of the modern, rather characterless structure, but has been very skilfully concealed behind a yellow plastic grit container.

On the way between Gartness and Drymen, I was becoming conscious that I would soon be leaving this lush countryside and moving into rather wilder terrain. On the high ground, a mere turn of the head changed the scene from comfortably pastoral to remote and rugged. In the distance the Highland peaks begin to assert them-selves, and in the foreground lies Conic Hill, which would be my first uphill slog.

The West Highland Way by-passes the village of Drymen, but as the place is one of my old stamping-grounds, I made a detour to have a look round. Drymen is an attractive, spotlessly clean and rather well-to-do place. People who can afford it like to move out here from Glasgow, and a fairly successful friend of mine called Billy Connolly lived here for a time. I remember the square in Drymen when it didn't

Drymen Square

look quite so perjink* as it does today. It was a great meeting-place in the old days for the bikers, hikers, scramblers and ramblers. They would lie around here on the grass of the square, recounting their heroic escapades, small fry like me hanging on every word. Bryan Chambers of Nevisport has a saying which goes, 'Home is the sailor, home from the sea, and the climber home from the pub'. I think there was quite a lot of that in Drymen. More talk than rock; and there was a song which I think illustrates the point rather neatly. Here's as much as I can remember.

The Bar-Room Mountaineers

In Drymen square, so fair and fine,
There stands a shop that sells good wine;
It's full of whisky, rum and beer,
For the bar-room mountaineers.
  CHORUS
  You can come and look us over,
  We are very seldom sober;
  And when we've had enough for four,
  You'll never find us on the floor;
  For it's up to the bar and ask for more,
  We're the bar-room mountaineers.

We've never climbed a great big hill,
And I hope tae God we never will;
For the highest we've climbed is a windae sill,
We're the bar-room mountaineers.
  Chorus
When you hear a tally-ho
In the middle of the night;
Don't tremble so, dear hostelite,
Just close your eyes and have no fear;
For it's only a drunken so and so,
He's a bar-room mountaineer.

* *perjink*: spruce, neat and tidy

Beginner's Hill

On leaving Drymen, I headed for the Forestry Commission car-park, and the start of the walk through the Garadhban Forest (pronounce it Garavan.) This is a beautiful part of the walk, on good forestry tracks, and the trees are not limited to the all-too-common gloomy ranks of regimented spruce. I was on a concert tour in Israel in 1968 when the great gales hit the West of Scotland. Friends told me what they had read of it, but it was only after I had been back for some time that I began to realise the extent of the damage. Thousands of acres of trees were destroyed, but it is due to the clearance caused by those winds that the Garadhban Forest offers such a variety of growth, and consequently, of wildlife. All the usual birds are to be seen, but one species which I couldn't quite see in the high tops of the conifers, but which I identified by sound alone, was the siskin. I used to breed them in aviaries, and their calls were very familiar to me. They are often seen here, as elsewhere, in the company of redpolls. The little goldcrest is common in the forest, and you are much more likely to hear, than see, the huge capercaillie as it goes blundering through the trees like a flying sofa. Even more exotic is the crossbill, especially the male, with his rosy red plumage. There is much to interest botanists,

Entering the Garadhban Forest

though I am sometimes puzzled by their seeming obsession with the rarities. It seems to me that some of the common plants are just as attractive, and certainly just as interesting. The humble cowslip, for instance, was used as a skin lotion, makes a lovely golden wine, and the juice from the flowers was recognised as a soothing potion for the nerves. It's common knowledge that the foxglove gives digitalis, used in the treatment of heart ailments, but when a chemical synthetic substitute was produced, it was discovered after a time to be inferior to the natural product, and the old foxglove came back into favour. Wood sorrel, which we used to nibble as children, has a peppery tang, and is even now sometimes used in salads, and as a sauce with fish dishes. It is believed that it was the wood sorrel, and not the shamrock, which it closely resembles, which St Patrick used to illustrate the concept of the Holy Trinity. This is another of those plants with a seed pod which explodes, shooting the seeds several yards; and for this reason, it is sometimes known as 'Sling fruit'.

The Garadhban Forest walk ends at a high fence with a stile, and the walker is abruptly on to open moorland. The knobbly bulk of Conic Hill rises before you, concealing the village of Balmaha on Loch Lomond. There were a few complaints about the way-marking on this stretch in the first season after the opening of the Way, but I'm afraid I am in no position to comment on this, as I simply took a line from the edge of the forest and headed straight for the hill. The whole concept of way-marking has caused some controversy, especially when the footpath was first being established: the diehards among the outdoor fraternity taking the view that walkers should rely on knowledge gained by experience, and that they should be able to use map and compass. Others objected to the marking-posts themselves as a kind of visual pollution. The posts are, in fact, a rather unobtrusive dark brown, and bear the Countryside Commission for Scotland's footpath symbol of a hexagon containing a thistle.

After crossing the moor, and negotiating the Burn of Mar, which I did by means of stepping stones, having abandoned the footpath and its bridge, I started on Conic Hill. The hill is about a thousand feet, but it's fairly steep, and the going is rough and heathery. One of the more ridiculous songs in the Scottish 'heather and haggis' repertory is a composition called 'Marching Through the Heather'. One stumbles, barges, or hirples* through heather. Marching is out of the question. I think a geologist would find Conic Hill interesting, for it seems to be composed of a kind of pudding of bluish-red sandstone,

* *hirples*: limps

Above At the Mar Burn *Below* Loch Lomond from Conic Hill

shot through with stones and pebbles of a quite different material. As you make your way up the steep slope, you realise that Conic Hill is not conical at all, though it appears so from the viewpoint at the edge of the Garadhban Forest. It is, in fact a ridge over a series of humpbacks, and the line of this ridge carries out into the waters of Loch Lomond in a string of islands. This spine, formed by the hill and the

Endrick Marshes from Conic Hill

islands marks the Highland Boundary Fault, recognised by geologists as the division between Highlands and Lowlands.

My painful, peching* progress to the summit of the hill was rewarded by a truly superb spectacle. The air was clear, the warmth of the sun was tempered by a fine breeze, and my pleasure in completing the modest little climb was vastly increased by a look over my shoulder. Across the moor lay the dark trees of the Garadhban Forest, and away beyond that, the Campsie hills, the mound of Dumgoyne, and the view back down the Blane valley. But the satisfaction of having covered that ground was more than matched by the anticipation of what lay ahead. Below lies the mouth of the River Endrick, and the nature reserve of the Endrick marshes, where one of Scotland's famous outdoor men, Tom Weir, does a lot of his bird-watching. The rich pickings of the marshes attract hosts of migratory birds, with their attendant predators. The osprey is seen on the loch, and Tom Weir tells me that a spoonbill, obviously an escapee from some zoo or bird garden, lived quite happily there for a time. Almost in line with the ridge of Conic Hill and its continuing string of islands, are the Arran Peaks, clearly visible through the glasses, and further to the north-west, the Luss hills and the Arrochar Alps. The great bulk of Ben Lomond suddenly seemed startlingly close on this diamond-clear day, and the scatter of islands lay in sharp chiaroscuro on the

* *peching*: panting

glittering waters of Scotland's famous loch. The walker will soon be following the loch shore, quite close to some of the islands, but the

Above Woods above Balmaha *Below* Woodland path to Balmaha

Inchcaillach from Balmaha

ridge of Conic Hill is a good place to consult the map and identify some of the main ones. All but one of the island names are prefixed by the ancient word for island: inch, or insh. In most parts of the West Coast of Scotland, the Gaelic form, *eilleann* is used. Continuing the ridge-line of Conic Hill is the high wooded bulk of Inchcaillach, and the smaller islands of Torrinch and Creinch. The islet to the left of Inchcaillach is Clairinch. Inchcaillach means the island of the old woman, and it is said that a nunnery was established there by St Kentigerna, who died on the island in AD 734. A few years ago, I went with the television cameras to the island's ancient graveyard, where lie some of the wild men of the McFarlane and Macgregor clans who competed for control of the area around Loch Lomond. The Macgregors are more often cast as the villains, but at one time the nocturnal exploits of the McFarlanes were so well known, that the moon itself was known as McFarlane's lantern.

I made my way carefully down the end of the ridge, and on to a rough, bracken-enclosed path which took me to the stile at the edge of the woods above Balmaha. All that remained was a pleasant, sun-dappled walk through the trees and down into the village. Balmaha, though small, is a bustling place in the tourist season, and is a very good place for the walker to stock up. For about the next twenty miles, you will be walking on Loch Lomond side.

Balmaha and the Bonny Banks

In Balmaha, I indulged myself with a proper meal, at a real table, with a real table-cloth; had a wash and relaxed in the village for half an hour or so, before going off to conduct an interview with a very charming lady called Mrs McFarlane. Margaret McFarlane has been running the busy boat-yard since the death of her husband Alex. Alex McFarlane was not only responsible for the yard, but also took the mail to the islands all over the loch; and some years earlier, as part of a BBC television series, he had taken my old singing partner Robin Hall and me on one of his regular trips. It was a delightful day out for us, and made a fascinating programme, and I was very happy that Margaret had decided to keep the boat-yard in the McFarlane family. Alex McFarlane had an encyclopaedic knowledge of the loch and its surroundings; he told some great fishing stories, and of times when the loch was so deeply frozen that horses and carts were taken from one side to the other. I also had a very interesting chat with a young botanist at the Ben Lomond Nursery. This was Sheila Grant, who filled in some of the woeful gaps in my knowledge of the flora of Loch Lomond side.

When I mentioned to my friends in Glasgow that I was to undertake this walk, I rather naively expected encouragement, possibly a little envy, even admiration: 'Good for you, James, we're sure you're the man for the job'. What I got was rapier wit. 'Are you sure this is prudent at your age?' and, 'What? Not with those wee legs?' and, 'Do you think the BBC would pay me to push your wheelchair?' and so on, and so on. But here I was, well on my way, with not a popped ligament or a cardiac arrest in sight. Feeling great, in fact. Enjoying myself enormously, and looking forward to the next section of the Way.

Loch Lomond really is a very remarkable place. On the west shore is the A82 trunk road which takes traffic into the West Highlands. On the east side, the road is a fairly modest affair after Balmaha, and peters out entirely at Rowardennan, leaving the wilderness area to the north accessible only to those who are prepared to hoof it. The loch is one of the longest in Scotland (23 miles), and is the greatest stretch of inland water in Britain. As is clear from the summit of Conic

Hill, the southern and northern aspects of the loch are quite different. As the great glacier which created it moved down from the ice-fields to the north, it gouged a deep cleft between the mountains, gradually slowing down and spreading out, so that the land around the lower reaches is gentle and fertile, and the loch itself wide, fairly shallow, and dotted with islands. To the north, the steep banks continue down to great depths – over six hundred feet off Inversnaid. The fertile land to the south was settled and farmed, though it was continually harassed by the wild clans from the north. The widely varying terrain around Loch Lomond, of marsh, shingle, woodland, arable land, mountain and moor, provide habitat for an astonishing variety of plants, insects, birds and mammals. Dr Agnes Walker of Glasgow's Kelvingrove Museum and Art Galleries tells me that about twenty-five per cent of all Britain's plants are found in the area. Life in the loch itself is equally diverse. There are salmon, brown and sea trout, eels, perch, some formidable pike and a strange wee beastie called a powan. The powan is a kind of fresh-water herring, and the theory is that its salty ancestors were trapped in the loch long ago. They appear to have adapted rather well, and are present in some numbers. Fishing friends tell me that though undoubtedly nutritious, they don't really taste of anything much.

My progress along the loch side was, I must confess, rather slow, because there was so much to see, and I met so many interesting people. So will you, I hope, and if you're not Scottish, ignore Sir Walter Scott's example, and do not refer to Loch Lomond as a lake. We have only one lake in Scotland, the Lake of Menteith, given its misnomer by the early Dutch map-makers, who misinterpreted the Scottish word *laich*, or *laigh*, meaning low, or low-lying, as lake. If you are interested in wildlife, a trip to Inchcaillach would be worthwhile before taking off on the loch side stretch. The island is now part of an official nature reserve, and very well cared for, though I remember it as a very noisy and busy place at times. Because of its accessibility from Glasgow, Balmaha became a meeting-place for a crowd of people whom we knew as the Balmaha cowboys. They would come out for the weekend in draped suits and winkle-picker shoes, much to the disgust of the 'real' weekenders. What offended us even more, was that they seemed to have a terrific time, with ample supplies of food and drink, girl friends, and accordions and guitars. They used to cross over to Inchaillach in horrifyingly overladen boats, and their carousing through the night could be heard for miles along the loch shore. Those days are long gone, however, and Inchcaillach is now left to the wild creatures, the McFarlane and Macgregor graveyard, and to rather more serious visitors.

Woodland and Water

Heading north from the old pier at Balmaha, (where I watched a delighted visitor from Yorkshire landing a six-pound sea trout). I was quickly on my way, on the rocky footpath around the loch shore. From now on, each step seems to bring Ben Lomond appreciably closer. Every turn in the path presents a change of scene, and the wooded shoreline recedes into the distant narrows of the loch. As I made my way around towards Milarrochy Bay, I noticed a big, bearded lad working on the shore with a group of youngsters. This was Steve Nunn, a countryside ranger, with special responsibility for the West Highland Way. I introduced myself, and suggested to Steve that the Loch Lomond side stretch must keep him pretty busy. He informed me that his beat in fact extended from Milngavie to Bridge of Orchy, a distance of about sixty miles. Steve and his charges, a cheery bunch of kids on a youth opportunities scheme, were busily clearing up litter on this lovely stretch of shore, and seemed fairly philosophical about the fact that people will come to a place like this

The old pier, Balmaha

and leave their garbage behind them. Steve accepts that the problem will be a continuous one, but is confident that continual propaganda and education will gradually reduce it to manageable proportions. I found it difficult to share his optimism, especially when he told me that people were actually uprooting the way-markers and using them for firewood.

There is a private campsite at Milarrochy Bay, and the Way takes briefly to the road, where I was amazed to see three girls carrying heavy packs, walking shoulder to shoulder on the wrong side of the road, and taking up as much width as a large car. It is obviously common sense (and common practice) to walk on the right side, facing the traffic; then, even if drivers don't see you, you see them, and conversation *can* be carried on by walkers in single file. After a short if, for some people, hazardous, stretch on the road, the Way takes off to the right into the Queen Elizabeth Forest Park. The walking is quite varied here, sometimes on open ground, at one point in the semi-darkness of a spruce plantation, and then through much more pleasant, deciduous woodland.

In the Queen Elizabeth Forest I spoke to Jim Denholm of the Forestry Commission, who told me that planting first started in the area in 1951, though they inherited some of the old-established oak woods which used to be worked by the Duke of Montrose's estate. Jim Denholm assured me that the Forestry Commission's 3,000 acres, (plus some more ground on Ben Lomond), carried a variety of

First steps on Loch Lomond side

conifers and not just the ubiquitous spruce which worries so many people; and it's true that from the other side of the loch, this diversity can be observed, especially in autumn when the larches change colour. The West Highland Way traverses a lot of Forestry Commission property, and Jim expressed some concern about campers who hide themselves away in thickly overgrown areas. They are in some danger during the periodic cull of the roe deer, and while it may be difficult for a marksman to mistake a camper bending over a stove for a roe deer, the camper may not be seen at all until it's too late. The moral is – ask permission before camping.

The first-time visitor to Loch Lomond may be surprised that the woodlands are predominatly oak, but in fact these trees have been so long associated with the area that they can now be considered native. Since the fifteenth century they have been used, firstly for house- and ship-building, and then as charcoal for iron-smelting. The old smelting sites, known as bloomeries, are found all along the loch shore. It has to be remembered, by the way, that there were settlements all around the Loch Lomond shores in earlier times. Later, the bark of the oak trees became important, as it was used in the process of tanning leather, and this is when the system of coppicing came into use. Coppicing was a kind of pruning system which encouraged continual new growth, and allowed maximum exploitation of the crop. Originally the oak forests were native sessile oak, and it was later that the English pedunculate oak was

Entry to Queen Elizabeth Forest

introduced. The two species have now almost totally hybridised, and with the native birch, alder, holly and rowan, provide a superb habitat for a wide variety of wildlife.

The route from Balmaha to Rowardennan offers the walker a constant change of scene, from shore to woodland and hill, and it's on this stretch that you'll pass the last of the bigger islands. This is Inchlonaig, which is famous for its yew trees. These are said to have been planted by Robert the Bruce, to ensure a supply of longbows for Scotland's archers. A little further north, you may see the remains of one of the famous Loch Lomond crannogs. The crannogs are man-made islands dating from the Iron Age, and they are composed of logs, stones and brushwood submerged in the loch. They were places of refuge, approached by cleverly constructed causeways or stepping stones. They are found in many parts of Scotland, some of them just large enough to be used in emergencies, and others able to support small settlements. They are being closely studied, and it is found that the underwater conditions preserve even organic materials used in woven baskets, footwear and clothing.

Near Rowardennan I met David Barber, whom I had first encountered near Craigallion Loch. He had recently graduated from Glasgow University and, in common with so many others, he found that his education and talents appeared to be of no value. He was filling his time inexpensively by walking the West Highland Way. We chatted for a while, mostly about the irony of the fact that it was the *first* great Depression that had brought so many working-class people to the outdoors all those years ago, and that history seemed to be repeating itself in detail. I wished him luck on the walk, and with his career, and we made our separate ways to Rowardennan.

Opposite Rowardennan Youth Hostel

Big Ben and the Old Man of the Loch

Rowardennan is an attractive and popular place, with a good hotel and a superb youth hostel, and if you have the time, it's worth making a stopover here, to climb Ben Lomond. The mountain is, at 3192 feet, far short of Ben Nevis at the end of your walk, but in good weather the walk to the summit ridge and back makes a great day out. Take the proper gear, and if you're inexperienced, don't go alone. If the weather is at all doubtful, forget it. Ben Lomond is perfectly safe, but only if one sticks to the footpath.

Two years before I walked the Way, I decided to spend my birthday on the Ben. That auspicious occasion falls on the tenth of March and there was, of course, snow on the tops. I started off in a light drizzle, but by the time I had cleared the trees, the rain had stopped and I was able to strip to the waist, continuing like this to well above the snow line, in brilliant sunshine. The snow was crisp and at first only a few inches deep, but quite soon I was well-wrapped again, and slogging through soft new falls which were more than knee-deep. The going was hard, but it was fine to look back at the long line of my footprints, leading the eye back down to where the islands studded the coruscating surface of the loch. The snow became deeper and deeper as I climbed, but it was a fresh fall and a serious decrease in visibility which forced me to turn back, only about forty-five minutes from the top. I was disappointed not to have reached the summit, but it was a wonderful day.

The Ben Lomond footpath begins immediately opposite the Rowardennan hotel, and is marked by an antique petrol pump. This reminder of times past is an attractive and interesting object, but it is being sadly neglected. I don't know who, if anyone, is responsible for its care, but it would be a pity to let it rot away. Equally interesting is the plaque on the wall of the hotel, which says:

A REQUEST FROM THE HOLIDAY FELLOWSHIP

Friend, when you stray, or sit and take your ease,
On moor, or fell, or under spreading trees,
Pray, leave no traces of your wayside meal,
No paper bags, no scattered orange peel,
Nor daily journal littered on the grass,
Others may view these with distaste, and pass.
Let no one say, and say it to your shame,
That all was beauty here before you came.

These words, printed on a card, price 2d. can be obtained from the Holiday Fellowship Ltd. 'Highfield,' Golders Green Road, London, N.W.11.

Below left Old pump and footpath to Ben Lomond at Rowardennan
Below right Leaving Rowardennan

The walker will probably find this stretch between Rowardennan and Inversnaid the roughest part so far, but it is absolutely fascinating. There is no striding along here, but a great deal of scrambling over, under and between huge crags. There are sections on the rough shore-line, and leafy walks through the oak and birch which dominate the woodlands. Sometimes the path is barely wide enough for your boots, and the rocks drop away by your left foot to the dark-brown water below. Bird life abounds, and it was here that I heard the maniacal cackle of the green woodpecker, known in some parts of England as the 'yaffle' because of its call. It was here, too, that a tiny movement caught my eye, only inches from the path and the boots of Way-walkers, and a very anxious willow-warbler began to flit among the branches a few yards from my head. A brief search revealed the perfect little nest; a domed structure with its entrance placed at the side. In the downy, feather-lined cup, five newly-born nestlings raised their naked heads, with bulging blind eyes and gaping, hungry beaks. Incredible to think that in a few short months these tiny scraps of life would fly as far as North Africa to escape the rigours of the Scottish winter.

If you keep your eyes open after you have negotiated the stretch of pathway through a conifer plantation, you will see, between the track

Rain on Loch Lomond

Cuilness

and the loch shore, the Rowchoish bothy. This is a stone-built
structure with a good, sound roof and it was restored by the Scottish
Rights of Way Society, with the help of the Forestry Commission as a
memorial to William Ferris, a pioneer in Scottish outdoor move-
ments. The path continues to twist and turn, dip and climb,
occasionally opening up to offer views over the loch, which are the
more pleasing by their unexpectedness. Along this stretch you'll have
sightings of Ben Arthur, known to generations of Scottish climbers as
'The Cobbler', and on a clear day, several of the main peaks on your
route can be identified.

A little way on from Rowchoish bothy, the track emerges from the
trees, crosses the Cuilness burn by a wooden footbridge and comes
into an open area with a shingly shore, and, a few yards up the slope to
the right, a very attractive little house. This is Cuilness farm, where I
met one of the most interesting people I was to encounter on the whole
route. This was John Groome, a tall, quietly-spoken man who had
lived in the splendid isolation of Cuilness for fourteen years. I asked
him whether he found the West Highland Way (which passes within
yards of his door) an intrusion, and he told me that, much as he loves
his solitude, he likes to see people enjoying the Way, and that he found
most of them very caring and responsible. John is in his seventies, but
he has the awareness and enthusiasm of a highly intelligent child. I
mentioned to him that I had spotted a dipper's nest under the

Wild Goat

footbridge on the Cuilness burn, and he immediately told me when the first egg was laid, the size of the clutch, the incubation period, and when the young had flown. John's sitting-room was long on bachelor comfort, and very short on obsessive tidyness, the walls covered in wildlife prints and his own delightful water colours. This remarkable man (he celebrated his seventieth birthday with an ascent of the Ben the hard way, by the Cuilness burn), keeps a journal in which he records all his observations of the local wildlife; the whole thing illustrated by his own delicate colour drawings. He has even managed to tame some of the famous Loch Lomond wild goats, which, as they feed along the tangled shore, most people are lucky just to glimpse. John used to spend a part of each day clearing up litter between the house and Inversnaid, and he's very encouraged by the fact that although there are now many more people in the area, they are, in fact, becoming more responsible and leaving less rubbish than before. He has saturated the area around Cuilness with nesting boxes of various types, over the years, and when I spoke to him, there were more than a dozen pairs of pied flycatchers nesting between the house and Inversnaid. John Groome has now left Cuilness, and is living in the village of Gartocharn, still close to his beloved Loch Lomond.

A road has now been bulldozed over the hill and down to the little house at Cuilness, making a scar which can be seen from the other side of the loch, and representing the first breach of the Craigrostan shore since Rob Roy's time. Everyone respects the local farmers' need and right to make a living, but there is concern that the making of this road affects so many people. An even greater threat to the integrity of the area is the proposed Craigrostan scheme, which would be Britain's biggest pumped-storage hydro complex. This would involve building a reservoir on the north-western slopes of the Ben, and an underground power station on the lower slopes. The whole wilderness area would be irrevocably altered; the construction process alone causing great upheaval. The project is currently postponed, but not cancelled. Anyone wishing to learn more about the project, and indeed about any of the many problems facing the Loch Lomond area, should contact the Friends of Loch Lomond. This dynamic group has the interests of the Loch Lomond area and the people who live and work there, very much at heart. It is headed by a totally committed and hard-working lady called Hannah Barr-Stirling who will be pleased to hear from anyone who is interested in the well-being and future of Loch Lomond. Her address is on page 94.

As I left Cuilness for Inversnaid, I saw a final little illustration of John Groome's personality. By a tiny burn he had knocked in a post, on which he had hung a tin drinking cup. His humanity, however, was tempered by realism. He had drilled a wee hole in the bottom.

Fish Tales and the Famous

Lord, suffer me to catch a fish
So large, that even I,
When talking of it afterwards,
May have no need to lie.

Arrival at Inversnaid comes as something of a surprise, as one emerges suddenly from the trees to cross the wooden footbridge high above the Arklet falls, and descend into the grounds of the hotel. The Arklet falls and the Snaid burn can be anything from a gentle trickle to a raging torrent; but this is common in the West Highlands. Spate or drought can transform everything. I was greeted at the Inversnaid Hotel by the owner, George Buchan; a courteous man with a dark-brown voice which would be the envy of any broadcaster. The hotel, which was originally owned by the Duke of Montrose, is over 150

The Arklet falls, Inversnaid

years old, and it has been in George Buchan's family for more than thirty years. George explained that the hotel's position at the only break in the hills on the east shore of the loch made it very important, and it was the most popular stopping-point on the old round-tours from Glasgow. Tourists would come by train to Balloch, then by steamer to Inversnaid, where they would join a horse-drawn coach for Loch Katrine. There was another steamer journey on Loch Katrine, then it was the coach again to Callander, and the train back to Glasgow. This was a one-day trip, and the horses worked from Inversnaid until 1936. George showed me a lovely old photograph of himself as a wee boy, with the coach and horses in the hotel yard.

The steamer at Inversnaid

Probably the most famous of all the famous visitors to Inversnaid were the Wordsworths, and George Buchan seemed quite intrigued that William's poem to 'A Sweet Highland Girl' (who was a waitress in the hotel) was written while his sister Dorothy was accompanying him. Here's part of it:

Nor am I loth, though pleased at heart,
Sweet Highland girl! from thee to part;
For I, methinks, till I grow old,
As fair before me shall behold,
As I do now, the cabin small,
The lake, the bay, the waterfall;
And thee, the spirit of them all!

What a gift to the tabloids, had they existed. 'Love looms as wordsmith Wordsworth woos waitress.' ' "Och, he chust fab, what-effer," breathed luscious leggy Loch Lomond lovely . . . '

I suggested to George that I might like to stay for the night, and he produced a tariff which seemed fairly reasonable. Bed 2/6d, Bath 1/6d, Breakfast 2/6d, and Dinner 4/6d. The bad news was that this was in 1930. I decided to stay anyway, and I'm glad that I did.

After a bath which was luxurious to the point of decadence, I had a meal and made my way to the bar, where I found myself in jolly company, talking to farmers, shepherds, gamekeepers and the like, and being talked at by Neil Jeffries. Neil, an affable kind of fellow who didn't seem to have any prejudices against conversation, informed me that he was the secretary of the most famous club in Scotland, namely the Inversnaid Angling and Boating Club. After the inevitable tales of shark-sized trout, and whale-sized salmon, Neil directed my attention to a fine mounted fish displayed above the bar. He chatted on about this specimen at some length before informing me that it had been caught in Maryhill Road, Glasgow. Even my suspicions were aroused by this, and a brief examination of the little plaque on the case told me that it was caught by Mr Neil Jeffries on the first of April. The fish, in fact, is a skilfully carved and painted wooden replica, which used to hang over a Glasgow fishmonger's shop. A very real fish Neil encountered was the large salmon which raced to the bottom of the loch after being hooked, and refused to move. After various attempts to get the salmon to run, a heavy padlock was threaded on to the line, and slid down to bump the fish on the nose. The only result was that the padlock became entangled with the hook, and the salmon made its escape. There is an open offer of a bottle of malt to anyone who returns to Neil Jeffries a salmon with a padlock!

Many fishing tales emanated from the bar of the Inversnaid Hotel, some dramatic, some daft. My own favourite concerns an angler who, in an excess of excitement at hooking a good fish, inadvertently projected his false teeth over the side and into ten feet of water. When the excitement had died down, one of the fishing party surreptitiously attached his own false teeth to his hook and lowered them into the

Inversnaid from the west shore

water. Great were the feigned cries of astonishment when the teeth were hauled in, but when they were handed to the toothless one, he examined them briefly, observed, 'Naw, they're no' mine,' and casually tossed them back over the side.

The fishermen at Inversnaid were unanimous in bemoaning the fact that the number of salmon in Loch Lomond has been diminishing for a variety of reasons. They told me that the salmon gain access to the loch by way of the River Leven, and there is so much netting and poaching that, to be sure of making it to the loch, a salmon has to catch the bus at Balloch and get off at Inverbeg.

The Eagle and the Outlaw

The mountains of Ben An and Ben Venue are really very grand,
Likewise the famous and clear silvery strand,
Where the bold Rob Roy spent many a happy day,
With his faithful wife, near its silvery bay.

The silvery bay is Loch Katrine, and these finely-honed lines are by the great William Topaz McGonagall, poet and tragedian.

Above the Inversnaid Hotel, a farm now occupies the site of the old Garrison which was built there in 1719. Its main purpose was to contain the wild Macgregors, who had held these lands since they were ousted from Glenorchy and Glenstrae by the expansionist Campbells. The Macgregors, characteristically, did not take this lying down, and before the barracks were even completed, they had kidnapped a group of the builders and taken them into the lowlands, where they were left to face a long walk back. Later, during the Jacobite uprising of 1745, the Macgregors actually occupied the barracks; a bold action which had serious repercussions for them when the rebellion failed.

By far the most famous, and certainly the most troublesome, of all the Macgregors was Robert Macgregor, or Rob Roy. The word Roy comes from the Gaelic word for red, and referred to the flaming hair and beard of the villain/hero, outlaw/saviour. The man certainly ranks with Burns, Bruce, Bonnie Prince Charlie, and Wallace as an authentic Scottish folk hero. His life and times have been wildly romanticised, most writers taking their cues from Walter Scott, and from *Highland Rogue*, written by Daniel Defoe, and published in 1723. I am lucky enough to own a beautifully-bound copy of a more interesting account of Macgregor's life; *Rob Roy and His Times* published by Kenneth Macleay in 1818. A recent, and even finer book, which explodes many of the myths, and demonstrates that the true story is much more extraordinary than any existing fictionalised version, is *Rob Roy Macgregor, His Life and Times* by the Scottish writer and climber, W. H. Murray. Dr Murray's book is richly textured and deeply researched, giving a detailed and fascinating picture of life in the Scottish Highlands in Rob Roy's time.

> *The eagle he was lord above,*
> *And Rob was lord below!*

William Wordsworth's lines hardly overstated the case. For a time, even in adversity, Rob Roy Macgregor reigned supreme here. He is commonly depicted as an outlaw, but there is little doubt that he was a man more sinned against than sinning. The odd bit of sinning didn't appear to bother him unduly, however. Rob Roy was the nephew of the fifteenth chief of the clan Gregor, and he was a man whose great physical strength and agility were matched by courage and independence of spirit. All this, combined with a good education and a widespread reputation for shrewdness in his business dealings, made him a pretty formidable adversary for those who were envious of the lands and power of the Macgregors. For a time, Campbell of Argyll, and the Duke of Montrose, who were great rivals, vied for the support of Macgregor, and when Rob Roy took the name of Campbell (the Macgregor name being proscribed by law), Argyll took it as a personal tribute. In fact, Rob Roy's mother's name was Campbell.

Kenneth Macleay's book has a very fine woodcut which purports to be a portrait of Rob Roy Macgregor, but it is well established that no likeness was taken during his lifetime, though he was described in much detail after his death. He was said to have been about middle, or slightly below middle height, the average for the Highlander of the time being about five foot six inches. Even among the tough mountain people, his physique was exceptional, with a deep chest, and almost freakishly broad shoulders. His legs, which were thickly covered in red hair, were massively muscled. Like his fellow clansmen, Rob normally disdained the horse, and thought little of walking thirty miles of high rugged country in a day. From boyhood, he developed his skills with the weapons of the day, and his formidable talent with the broadsword was enhanced by long and extremely powerful arms. He was only twice bested in combat; once by a trick, and once in his old age, and it was said that he never sought a fight, and never killed, except when that conclusion was unavoidable.

Rob Roy was born at Loch Katrine in 1671 and, while still a very young man, had established a flourishing and wholly legitimate cattle business. At this stage of his career, his connections were perfectly respectable. His cousin was Dr James Gregory, professor of medicine at Aberdeen, and his father, Donald, was a Lieutenant in the Jacobite army, as well as chief of Clan Gregor. Rob Roy was deeply involved in the affairs of the time, and had a close association with the Duke of Montrose in the cattle-trading business (the black Highland cattle were greatly in demand in the markets of the Lowlands and England); but when one of his drovers absconded with some funds, Montrose held Macgregor responsible. He demanded that Rob Roy should sign over his property until he could make good the loss, but when Macgregor did eventually raise the money, he found that interest, expenses, and various legal devices had been used to thwart him, and he himself was dispossessed. Montrose later went further, ordering the eviction of Rob Roy's family, and the burning of his house. Macgregors's outlawry was now confirmed, and his war of attrition against Montrose began.

There are many more stories of Rob Roy's exploits than those invented by Walter Scott, and it appears that he is not known as the Scottish Robin Hood without cause. When Montrose's factor was about to evict a widow for failing to pay arrears of rent, Macgregor gave the woman the money from his own pocket. He then waited until she had paid, and waylaid the drunken factor under cover of darkness. The woman had her house, rent paid, and Rob had his money back.

On another occasion, returning from Carlisle, he witnessed the hanging of four men by some soldiers. When the officer in charge then ordered his men to throw a young girl into the river, bound hand and foot, Rob Roy protested. He was told, sneeringly, to be on his way, before he suffered a similar fate. In seconds, several militiamen were struggling in the water, the officer and two men were dead, and the remaining soldiers were in flight.

Rob Roy eventually submitted to General Wade, and was pardoned in 1726, although there is no doubt that his seeming capitulation was decided by expediency rather than weakness. Rob

Roy Macgregor, after a wild and turbulent life of violence and hazard, died peacefully in his bed at Balquhidder. His last words were, 'It is all over. Put me to bed. Call the piper. 'Let him play *Cha till mi tuille.'*

Rob Roy Macgregor had five sons. They were James, Robin, Coll, Ranald and Duncan. Robin fought with the detested Duke of Cumberland at the battle of Fontenoy, was a known murderer, and was eventually hanged for the crime of abduction. James, in contrast, fought as a Major in the rising of 1745 with Bonnie Prince Charlie, was responsible for the daring destruction of the barracks at Inversnaid, and distinguished himself at the battle of Prestonpans, and at Culloden. He was imprisoned, but escaped to die in poverty in Paris.

Weeds and the Wilderness

When Gerard Manley Hopkins visited this area in the late nineteenth century, he wrote a poem which ended:

What would the world be, once bereft
Of wet and wildness? Let them be left,
O let them be left, wildness and wet;
Long live the weeds and the wilderness yet.

He need have had no worries about this part of Loch Lomond. Although the Countryside Commission for Scotland has forced its little footpath through here, the weeds and the wilderness still prevail. I was told that this would be the toughest part of the Way, and indeed, the going is not easy, but I remember coming here as a teenager, and having to wrestle and hack my way through yard by yard. The clearing of fallen trees and undergrowth, and the provision of some kind of path has been a tremendous task; and of course, the Way here will require constant maintenance. The weeds and wilderness are poised to take over again. The Loch is much narrower at this point, but although the walker is so close to the busy A82 on the west shore, the sense of primeval other worldliness is complete. Great bulging cliffs hang over your right shoulder, and in places, the path clings to steep rocks going down into the loch, which is fairly deep close by the shore at some points. There is no real danger, but take

* *'Cha till mi tuille'*: I shall return no more.

care. The variety and the density of the vegetation is indescribable, and the area teems with woodland birds. It was here that I had my first sighting of the pied flycatcher, a delightful little black and white bird which is colonising the east shore of Loch Lomond, and doing very well. A pair of mergansers were feeding off shore, and woodpeckers and tree creepers were everywhere. The tree creeper is a tiny, mouse-like bird; very beautiful at close quarters, but quite hard to spot. Once located, however, it is easy to observe, as it seems to completely ignore human beings as it explores the fissures in the bark of a tree for tiny insects. I've noticed that goldcrests will also feed, quite happily, a few feet from a quiet watcher. Even a tyro bird-watcher will get results in a place like this, by simply sitting down, shutting up, and keeping still.

I had been rather disappointed not to have seen the wild goats on the Rowardennan–Inversnaid stretch, but I was rewarded here with a close sighting of a feeding group which included a huge white billy. The Loch Lomond goats are long established, and are said to have been given the protection of Robert the Bruce after they had lain down in front of a cave in which he was hiding from his enemies. That certainly would have been an effective diversion, for they can be smelled at a distance of half a mile. There is a famous cave along here, among some huge boulders. It is known as Rob Roy's cave, but it is believed also to have sheltered Robert the Bruce, after his defeat at the battle of Dail Righ in 1306.

Going on through the tangle, and making my way through boulders the size of tenement buildings, I came on a burn running down over some steep slabs of rock and into the deep waters of the loch below. I decided to cross straight over this waterfall, as it was a warm sunny day, and I wasn't too concerned about getting wet. Half-way across, I wished I hadn't. I am no climber, and have a poor head for heights. The rock was very slippery, and I was aware that if I lost my foothold, nothing would stop me from ending in the loch about thirty feet below. My crossing was not made any easier by the fact that I continued to address my tape recorder on the way over, but I arrived at the other side without mishap. I enjoyed this little escapade, but it is not something I should advise. There is a steep path which goes away up the side of the burn, to cross a footbridge and descend on the other side.

The going eases up very soon after this, coming out on to a little shingly shore, before striking uphill towards the old buildings of

Doune. The last time I had seen these, they were in a sorry state; semi-derelict, and full of dead sheep in various stages of putrefaction. A treat for the hoodie crows, but not very inviting to the walker. I was pleased to see that the buildings had been restored, with new roofing and window frames, and gleaming white paint. They are in an idyllic situation here, on an open slope above the loch, and I must confess to some envy of whoever owns them. The walking is open and downhill from here to Ardleish farm, which marks the end of the Loch Lomond section of the West Highland Way. The path follows the slope up to the right of Ardleish farm, but I moved down to a little bay at the head of the loch for a snack, a brief rest, and a last look at the bonnie banks.

I hadn't seen a human being since Inversnaid, but suddenly it was the rush hour. Three young girls appeared. They were quite small, and carrying gigantic packs. They told me that they were engaged on a Duke of Edinburgh award scheme expedition. They chatted for a while, and drank most of my coffee, and as they made their way round the loch shore, dwarfed by their rucksacks, I wondered how they would make out in the tangle I had just finished. No sooner had they disappeared from view, than two lads came out on to the shingle from the Inversnaid end of the bay. They were a hardy-looking pair, and obviously fairly seasoned walkers. Because they were experienced, and came from outside Scotland, (from Newcastle and Warrington) I was interested in their impressions of the Way. They were lavish in their praise, and said it was the most beautiful and interesting walk they had done. They did not, however, enjoy the Scottish midges, and thought the way-marking was somewhat erratic. I had reason to remember their words a little further up the route.

Having cleared up my utensils, and cooled my feet in the icy cold waters of the loch, I started up the slope to the east of Ardleish farm. A lovely high walk takes you past the Dhu Lochan (the little black loch) and at the highest point, the peaks of Beinn Lui, Beinn Oss, and Beinn Dubhcraig (pronounced Doochray) are clearly visible. I strode down on this last stretch through the trees, to the flat ground which leads to the farm at the Beinglas burn, and promptly got lost.

A Highland Hotel and a Sad Song

The marking of the Way at this point was a trifle confusing (it has since been improved), and I made the mistake of doing what I was told, rather than relying on what I knew, with the result that I spent some time floundering aimlessly around on the wrong side of the Inverarnan canal. I discovered later that many of the Way-walkers went straight past the Beinglas farm, and found themselves half-way to Crianlarich when they had been aiming for Inverarnan. In fact, one turns left immediately after crossing the footbridge, to follow the footpath to the bridge over the River Falloch. The Inverarnan House Hotel is about a quarter of a mile south of the bridge; and a couple of miles down the road at Ardlui there is a railway station, a campsite, a shop and another hotel. Many walkers prefer to bypass this point, and press on for Crianlarich, but if you'd like a look at a real old Highland Hotel you should stop at Inverarnan.

The hotel caters for Way-walkers, and the owner, Duncan Macgregor, has been exposing and restoring the lovely old stone walls and opening up the big lounge, with its ancient, open fireplaces at each end. I spent the night there, and from my window I could look straight across to the Grey Mare's Tail – the falls on the Beinglas burn. They drop about a thousand feet in a thousand yards. In fine weather they look lacy and pretty, but in spate, they are a colossal, powerful rush of water. The Inverarnan Hotel was one of the key stopping places of the old cattle drovers. From here, they swung across the head of the loch and into Glengyle, on their way down to Perth, Crieff, Falkirk, and even down into England. Inverarnan later became one of the favourite watering holes of the well-to-do tourists of the nineteenth century, and the Inverarnan canal was constructed to allow them to continue from the head of the loch, almost to the back door of the hotel. The original owner of this hotel was a very famous and powerful one indeed, the Marquis of Breadalbane.

The Breadalbanes sprang from the Campbells who, of course, gave the Macgregors such a hard time, and for a period were the most powerful family in Scotland. Their estates stretched from Aberfeldy to Killin, through Glen Dochart to Ben Mohr and Crianlarich, then by Strathfillan to Bridge of Orchy, Loch Tulla and the Black Mount.

Above Coire Ba *Below* View from Ba Bridge

They also had valuable holdings in Oban, and in Seil Island, where they owned the slate quarries at Easdale. The power conferred by such vast holdings is almost unimaginable; not only over peoples' livelihoods, but over their way of life, and even their ideas. Some years ago, when I was making a television programme on Loch Tay, an old fellow in the bar of the Kenmore Hotel recited a poem about the Breadalbanes. I wrote it down, and later, put a tune to it. Here's part of it:

> *From Kenmore to Ben Mohr,*
> *The land is a' the Marquis's;*
> *The mossy howes,**
> *The heathery knowes,**
> *An' ilka bonnie park is his.*

> *The bearded goats*
> *The toozie stots,**
> *An' a' the braxy* carcases;*
> *Ilk crofter's rent,*
> *Ilk tinker's tent,*
> *An' ilka collie's bark is his.*

> *The muircock's craw,*
> *The piper's blaw,*
> *The ghillie's hard day's wark is his;*
> *From Kenmore to Ben Mohr*
> *The warld is a' the Marquis's.*

The overweening power of the Laird (in this case, Colquhoun of Luss), is also illustrated by this proclamation from the pulpit of Luss kirk:

> *Oyez, oyez, oyez. There will be no Lord's day here next Sabbath,* *because the Laird's wife will have a muckle* washin', and she needs* *the kirk tae dry her claes in.*

At this point in my walk, I needed a song for my radio programmes, and could not find anything suitable in the traditional repertoire, so I decided to write one about Inverarnan. This was an area of great Jacobite activity in the past, and it occurred to me that we are always given the impression that every man who was at Culloden knew exactly why he was there, and was totally committed to his cause:

* *howes*: hollows *knowes*: knolls *toozie stots*: touzled steers *braxy*: disease of sheep *muckle*: big

but obviously they were there for a variety of reasons, and many of them died, as in other battles, because they had been caught up in the excitement of the times, and became victims of their own slogans.

The Braes o' Inverarnan

Dae ye mind how we roved, love,
On the braes o' Inverarnan,
On the Lomond's wild shores,
In the high summer time?
And little we thocht, love,
On the braes o' Inverarnan,
How soon cruel fate,
Oor twa herts wad twine.*

But a Prince won my hert, love,
And his cause, it stole my reason,
And the blood leapt and sang
Tae the pibroch's wild thrum:
So I kilted my plaidie,
Turned my back on Inverarnan.
And I marched far awa'
Tae the drub o' a drum.

But my eyes they grow dim now,
And my hert, it grows sae eerie,*
On the muir o' Culloden,
My face tae the rain;
And I mind on my love, now,
On the braes o' Inverarnan;
And I know that I never
Shall see her again.

© *Jimmie Macgregor*

The Breadalbanes kept the Inverarnan hotel as a teetotal establishment, but Duncan Macgregor has changed that, and there is now an air of great conviviality in the place. During my stay, I had the pleasure of introducing four charming Dutch girls who were walking the Way to the traditional Scottish malt. I also, I discovered much later, introduced them to the traditional Scottish hangover, and they made a rather late start from their campsite next morning!

---

* *twine*: part, separate   *eerie*: sad   *A Highland Hotel and a Sad Song* 61

I made a fairly early one, and was quickly over the bridge on the Falloch, across the field to the Beinglas farm, and on my way to Crianlarich.

Grannies and the Monstrous Regiments

A left turn at the Beinglas farm put me back on the Way, and heading north into Glen Falloch. For a while, the going was not too pleasant. Conditions underfoot were boggy and uneven, and the path enclosed and tangly. This soon opens out, however, as the walker enters the lower reaches of the glen, to follow the river bank. The River Falloch is very beautiful indeed, every turn revealing a new succession of deep brown pools, rushing creamy falls, and broad shallows. There is a real feeling of wildness on this stretch, yet at no time are you far from the main road and the West Highland Railway, which runs through the glen on its way to Mallaig. When the idea of a railway through here was first mooted, there was fierce competition between rival land-owners to grab what they could, and the struggle became quite nasty on occasions. The whole idea fizzled out, however, and it was to be many years before the now famous, and wonderfully scenic, West Highland Railway was built.

Glen Falloch marks the beginning of another distinct stage on the walk, with the country beginning to open out, and the views becoming wider and more spacious. There is now a noticeable increase in the number of Forestry Commission plantations which have become such a controversial feature of the Scottish landscape. What I've heard described as the 'monstrous regiments' of sitka spruce are displacing the sheep which once displaced the people in so many parts of the country. They have an interesting effect on the wildlife, however, as, when the trees are quite small, they become heavily undergrown with weeds and grasses which grow up around the roots and into the lower branches. This results in an influx of rodents, and with the rodents come the predators: the kestrels, buzzards, short-eared owls and harriers. Later, as the trees become a little taller, they are a haven for small birds – wrens, whinchats, warblers, robins, and the like, and at this stage, the plantation

In Glen Falloch

provides them with food, shelter, and nest-sites. The problems really begin as the trees approach maturity. The canopy closes over, light is almost totally excluded, the undergrowth dies out, and the forest floor becomes quite barren. The plantation is then a desert where wildlife is concerned, though one might find the odd carrion crow or buzzard nesting in the top branches, or an occasional small bird on the extreme edge.

Much more interesting are the Scots pines which are scattered along Glen Falloch. The Scots pine is Britain's only indigenous conifer, and the ones here in the glen are remnants of the old Caledonian forest which used to cover almost the whole of the north of Scotland. The Glen Falloch pines are gnarled specimens, sometimes split and broken by the weather, though there are some venerable granny pines which have survived everything. Everywhere are the sad remains of specimens which have succumbed, their tortured limbs reaching from the black peat like the bleached bones of dinosaurs. In the poor soil and hard climate, even granny trees of great age can be of fairly modest stature, but they are very imposing on the sky-line; looking like ancient monuments, which, in a very real sense they are. Many things put paid to the ancient forests of Scotland. Climatic changes, careless cropping, burning by early inhabitants as an action against wolves and bears, and later, by the English, as an action against the inhabitants. But in more recent times, the trees have been at greatest risk from the depredations of deer and sheep.

The Glen Falloch pines are the most southerly remnants of the old forest, though there is a very healthy wood a little further north in Glen Cononish, on the lower slopes of Ben Dubhcraig. These trees now enjoy the protection of a fence erected by the landowner, Major Cruikshank of Auchreoch. Landowners in Scotland generally get a pretty bad press, but there are examples of individual contributions to conservation. The Fleming family of the Black Mount area, for instance, are also fencing off sections of ancient forest.

Scots pines in Glen Falloch

In Glen Falloch, I spoke to Keith Graham, an energetic and dedicated Countryside Ranger with Stirling District Council, about the future of the Scots pines. He explained that the greatest danger now comes from cropping the seedlings by sheep and deer, so that natural regeneration is virtually impossible. Keith is involved in a scheme with the Scottish Wildlife Trust, which they call 'Plant a Pine'. In Glen Falloch, they have been concentrating on the two essentials: fencing and re-seeding. The seeds are gathered from the trees in the area, and the work is voluntary, but fencing is frighteningly expensive, so that all donations, however small, are useful. Keith's address will be found on page 94.

Proceeding up Glen Falloch, the Way leaves the river to cross under the railway by means of a cattle creep, and then over the main road. A short climb up the hill takes you on to an old track, and this is the first of the old military roads which you'll encounter as you head north. These roads were built by the English redcoats, and their main purpose was to subjugate people like me. Approaching Crianlarich, the walker again has a choice; a path which goes on to Tyndrum, or a little diversion into Crianlarich, with its shops, post office, railway station and Youth Hostel. I took the diversion, for I had an appointment with a very interesting man called Harry McShane.

Crianlarich Youth Hostel

Rituals and Rash Ramblers

Harry McShane, the warden at Crianlarich Youth Hostel, was a wiry, quiet-mannered man with very definite views on the West Highland Way: 'It should never have been, because it always was'. He explained this rather cryptic statement by pointing out that the main sections of the Way had always been accessible to keen outdoor people, and he felt that the way-marking, excessive publicity, and over-simplification of the problems, lured people on to the route who were not properly equipped for it. This seemed a rather gloomy picture to me, but Harry did have some real horror stories to back up his ideas. He told me that he had already taken more than fifty people off the Inverarnan to Crianlarich stretch, getting them across the river to the road, and up to the hostel by Land Rover. One rescue session lasted until four-thirty in the morning, and involved eighteen people whose average age was fifteen. A doctor was brought in carrying a seventy-pound pack, and wearing new boots. He spent four days in a hostel bed. A rather funnier story, though with serious overtones, concerned two fell runners from the south, who took to the high levels above Loch Lomond. These fellows were very hardy and experienced, but they were also very competitive, and became separated. It was only when the mist came down that they remembered that one was carrying the map, and the other the compass.

Harry accepted that most of these problems were to be expected in early days on the Way, and agreed with me that they were bound to diminish in time, but he stressed that many people were treating the walk too lightly, and felt that they should prepare themselves more thoroughly. His own enthusiasm for outdoor Scotland was unbounded, and his knowledge extensive. He told me an amazing story of a thousand-year-old ritual in the Crianlarich area, in which, to counter an ancient curse, two stone figurines are secreted in a cairn during the winter, brought out in the spring, and only replaced when the harvest has been completed. He assured me that this ritual was still being practised. As we parted, he invited me back to Crianlarich, promising to take me backpacking in his beloved hills. This was not to be. A few months after our meeting, Harry McShane died tragically.

The Way from Crianlarich re-joins the old military road, and makes its way through a plantation of mixed trees, and under the railway viaduct. An interesting feature on this part of the walk is the ruin of St Fillan's chapel. St Fillan was the son of St Kentigerna, who was associated with Inchcaillach on Loch Lomond, and gives his name to the river Fillan, and indeed the whole district of Strathfillan through which I was now walking. After passing Auchtertyre, the path comes back to the river at the Holy Pool, and this is a place which has pleasant memories for me. I used to stay quite regularly at the home of the Orr family, at Strathfillan church house, and Willie and Jan Orr's five children learned to swim in the pool. The pool has some more ancient associations, however, with St Fillan's bell, and a ritual cure for insanity. St Fillan's bell is now in the Edinburgh museum of antiquities, but it used to hang in the chapel here. The person whose mental stability was in question was immersed in the Holy Pool, then stripped naked, tied to a tombstone, and left in the chapel all night with the bell suspended over his or her head. It has been said that if the victim was not insane before this ordeal, he or she certainly would be after it. My own feeling is that anyone who accepted this load of old codswallop in the first place, was quite obviously a raving loony, and it's interesting that the sanity of the people who subjected others to this ordeal was never examined.

The River Fillan

Crossing the road at the bridge brings the walker immediately into an area known as Dail Righ, or King's Field, where Robert the Bruce took one of his few hammerings at the hands of the McDougalls of Lorne. If the walker wishes to go directly to Tyndrum, the route by the main road is a mere mile and a half, but the wildness of Glen Cononish should not be missed, with its views of Ben Lui, Ben Oss, and Ben Dubhcraig. I was glad I had chosen this route, for it was here that I saw a pair of peregrines wheeling high over my head, the sickle-shaped wings and spectacular flight quite unmistakable. I really needed to stock up on a few essentials at this point, but the day and the Way were so beautiful, that I was almost sorry to come down into the village of Tyndrum.

Entering Glen Cononish at Dail Righ

The House on the Ridge and Fair-haired Duncan of the Songs

Tyndrum, despite its small size, is quite an important place, standing as it does at the junction of the roads for Glencoe, Fort William and the north, and Oban and the islands to the north-west. The name Tyndrum derives from the Gaelic *Tigh an Droma* – the House on the Ridge – although I have heard it translated as the House of the Witch. The old bikers, hikers and climbers called it simply, 'the Drum'. The word *tigh*, or its English corruption *ty*, is often prefixed to Gaelic place names: *Tigh Beag*, for instance, meaning the Little House. Other Gaelic words which you will encounter all along the Way are *ben*, *bein* or *beinn*, meaning a mountain, and *sgor*, *sgurr*, and *stob*, meaning a peak; as in *Stob Ghabhar*, pronounced Stov Goe-err, the peak of the goats. *Dhu* is black, *glas* is grey, *bhan* is white, *buidhe* yellow. Where you see the word *craig*, or *creagh*, it means a rock or crag. *Creagh Dhu* is the black rock. *Lairig*, *lairg*, *lairige*, or *learg* is a high pass, so that the *Lairig Mhor* is the great high pass, and *Lochan na Lairig*, would be the little loch of the high pass. *Beinn Dhubhchraig* is the mountain of the black rock, and it's pronounced Ben Doo-chray.

Tyndrum is a good place to stock up, and in fact, is the last such facility until Kinlochleven, unless one is prepared to detour into Glencoe village. I remember the craft shop here when it was a simple wooden hut, but Derek and Lesley Wilkie and the Gosden family have built it up into a fine restaurant and craft centre, with a wide range of Scottish goods which rises well above the normal level of tourist bric-à-brac.

The little row of cottages opposite the filling station is known as Clifton, the name of the man who established the lead mines here. The ore was worked for about a hundred years, and as well as lead, yielded a little silver. The mine finally ceased production in 1862, but the scars of the old workings can still be clearly seen on the hill, as the walker moves up behind the village. Looking down on Tyndrum, it is easy to imagine how remote and desolate it must have been in earlier times, and it was here that Rob Roy made an escape which would have graced a really bad B-movie; making his exit through a rear window of the old inn, while his pursuers hammered at the front door. The track rises quite steeply on the far side of the village, to join the old military road which will take you to Bridge of Orchy, and indeed, virtually to the end of the Way. The track is good here, the walking is unrestricted and you can really stride along, in what feels like fine open, wild country. In fact, you are in sight of the main Glencoe road and the railway, all the way along here, but the buzzards are wheeling and crying overhead, the piratical-looking black and grey hooded crows are much in evidence, and everywhere are the meadow pipits – the heather linties, which we saw away back at Milngavie.

By far the most spectacular landmark on the way to Bridge of Orchy is the towering, near-perfect cone shape of Beinn Dorain, and nearby is the birthplace of the man who immortalised it in verse. This was Duncan Ban McIntyre, known to the Gaels as Fair-Haired Duncan of the Songs. He was also called, less meaningfully I think, the Highland Burns. McIntyre was born at a place called Druimliart in 1724, and unlike Burns, who was a well-educated man for his time and class, the Highland poet was quite illiterate – his work was transcribed from the spoken word by others. His poem on Beinn

Dorain is recognised as a masterpiece, and is especially moving when one remembers that it was written after he had moved to Edinburgh, and knew that he would probably never see the Highlands again. Duncan Ban McIntyre's work is loved by Highland people, and even in translation his devotion to the country manifests itself very powerfully. Although he was a stalker and shepherd, he hated what the sheep had done to Scotland in displacing the people, and he even wrote a poem in praise of the fox because it preyed on the sheep. It seems a pity to me that nothing more than a rickle* of stones mark his birthplace, though there is a rather unattractive monument at Dalmally.

At the Bridge of Orchy Hotel, I met the owners, Roddy McDonald, and his father, Angus, or, to give him his proper title, Eunas Thonnalach. I rather naively asked Eunas if he was acquainted with the works of Ban McIntyre, and he was half-way through the first verse of the Beinn Dorain poem before I had my tape recorder switched on. Roddy and Angus McDonald were catering splendidly for the Way-walkers, with specially constructed bunk-house accommodation, good drying facilities, and very low prices, and I'm happy to say that their successors, owner Stuart Bisset, and manager Peter Sutherland, have maintained and developed these facilities. The bunk-houses now have showers, there's a lounge with a log fire, good bar meals, and a very decadent artifact called a 'Foot Spa'.

Above The Duncan Ban McIntyre monument at Dalmally
Opposite Beinn Dorain

* *rickle*: heap, pile

Road-builders and a Road-mender

The old bridge behind the Bridge of Orchy Hotel was built by the English militia in 1751. Shortly beyond the bridge, the walker leaves the road to strike uphill to a point which gives yet another of those wonderful panoramic views which are a recurring, and exciting, feature of this walk. Although you are standing at just over a thousand feet, the eye takes in not only the desolation of the Rannoch moor, and the extent of the Black Mount, with the peaks of Ben Starav, Stob Ghabhar and Stob Coir an Albannach (known as Highlandman's peak), but over to the east, the great flat-topped bulk of Beinn Achaladair, and further over your shoulder, Beinn Dorain, and the Crianlarich hills, which you have now left behind. Before and below you lies lovely Loch Tulla, and the trees of Doire Darach*. The descent of the hill is quickly and easily done, bringing the walker to the old Inveroran Hotel. Inveroran competes with Kingshouse Hotel on Rannoch moor as the oldest inn site in Scotland, and I suppose everyone now knows that this is where Dorothy Wordsworth complained about her boiled eggs.

The Bridge of Orchy

* *doire*: clump, *darach*: oak-wood

Above Loch Tulla *Below* The Inveroran Hotel*

The Inveroran Hotel on a fine day is idyllic. There is a stream, an old stone bridge, ancient trees and little lawns, and the building itself appears to have grown there. From about the middle of the nineteenth century, tourists began to travel the length of Loch Lomond by steamer, then up through Glencoe and on to Fort William by horse-drawn carriage. Inveroran was an obvious and very welcome stop-over, but long before that, it was an important resting place for the cattle drovers on their long trek south. When the

* The Inveroran Hotel is now in the care of Lorna and Douglas Anderson, who are developing the facilities with the special requirements of way-walkers in mind.

Marquis of Breadalbane casually announced that Inveroran would be closed as a drovers' halt, as it interfered with his deer stalking, the cattlemen took out a lawsuit against him. In spite of the fact that the drovers' ringleader was a Macgregor, Breadalbane won his case. Not surprising, really, as there were rather more deer-stalkers than cattle-drovers among his friends in the House of Lords, where the decision was taken. People tend to think of areas like this as wilderness, but it should be remembered that until the failure of the forty-five rebellion, and the subsequent clearances of the Highlands, these places were well-populated, and farming was carried on very successfully. Every year, the drovers moved about seventy thousand sheep and around ten thousand cattle to the lowland and English markets, where dealers were glad to buy Highland stock.

The next section of the West Highland Way is one of the most exposed. It's wide open all the way down to Kingshouse, and there is not a stone or a tree for shelter. After a good first mile, I did it all in a downpour, and there was nothing for it but to get my head down and plod on. Fortunately, the track itself is good; a little broken up in places, but considering that it was laid in the 1700s it was not at all bad. The English military experience of the rebellions of 1715 and 1745 demonstrated rather painfully that, on their own ground, the Highlanders could run rings around the highly-trained and disciplined redcoats. The answer was obviously a system of roads which would enable troops to be moved quickly into troubled areas, and the man whose name is still associated with these superbly well-built roads and bridges is General George Wade. This is, in fact, a wee bit strange, for Wade was responsible for about two hundred miles of road, while the lesser-known William Caulfield, his successor, built around eight hundred miles. But then, Wade was a General, while Caulfield was a mere Major. The work was superb, however. Many of those roads are still in use, and modern roads often follow the routes of the original surveys.

The old military road takes you to Victoria Bridge then to Forest Lodge, a relic of the days when vast tracts of Scotland were given over to the sport of deer-stalking. The main features of this stretch are Coire Ba, Ba Bridge and Ba cottage. Coire Ba is a gigantic *coire*, or corrie, with great ridges running down to the lower levels. Ba Bridge crosses a little gully where the river rushes between upturned slabs of pinkish orange granite. Ba cottage is now a mere ruin on the old Glencoe road, but there is a man called Duncan Croall who

Above Inverarnan House Hotel *Below* The Grey Mare's Tail from
Inverarnan

remembers delivering papers here in an old car before the war. Duncan Croall worked for a time for the Breadalbanes who used to own this area, as they owned almost everything else. Working on a road gang on the estate in filthy wet weather, Duncan was the only man who failed to doff his cap in the traditional manner when Lady Breadalbane swished past. He meant no disrespect, he was simply busy, and very wet; but he was summoned the very next day and dismissed. A trivial enough incident, but perhaps it is by such attention to detail that power is maintained.

The Black Mount estate was eventually acquired by the Fleming family, and up on the moor to your left, as you reach the highest part of the track, you will see a stone monument. This is a memorial to Peter Fleming, the travel writer; brother of Ian who created the James Bond fantasies. One very soon arrives at the White Corries Ski Centre with its chair lift, and the track meets the road at Blackrock cottage. Moving downhill to the right, the walker crosses the main Glencoe road, to complete the short walk to the Kingshouse Hotel.

The Altnafeadh Rocking-chair and the Naming of the Bens

The Kingshouse Hotel is reputed to be the oldest inn in Scotland, but seems to be going to a lot of trouble to look like the newest. It's certainly very comfortable and well-appointed, and I'm sure it is greatly appreciated by the tourists who pass this way, but I take more pleasure from tradition than modernity in a place like this.

I remember the Kingshouse in less formal days when the hikers and climbers used it as a centre for their meetings and sing-songs. There were some great singers and fine songs, and even more terrible singers and dreadful songs, which were equally enjoyable. Kingshouse is undoubtedly a good central point from which to explore this fascinating area. The Rannoch moor is an awesomely impressive place, and a couple of walkers who had come up from the rich countryside of Kent told me that, to them, it felt like another planet. The moor extends to about sixty square miles, and is a wilderness of peat hags and lochans. The whole expanse was once covered by Scots pines, and thousands of them still lie in the bogs, preserved by the peat. This is a wildly beautiful place, but desperately bleak and potentially deadly in winter. The problems associated with the building of the railway here were formidable, and great credit must go to the people who planned and surveyed it, and to the men who did the hard physical work, sometimes in truly dreadful conditions. In some of the boggier parts of the moor, the railway was floated on beds of brushwood and timber, and in certain areas, the undulations of the track can be seen under the train.

From Kingshouse the Way moves down the glen to Altnafeadh and the Devil's Staircase, and it was near here, by the River Coupall, that I had arranged to meet Alan Thompson. Alan is a freelance photo journalist, and a townie who has settled happily in the Highland village of Ballachulish. From this centre, he pursues his walking, climbing, cycling and pot-holing, and writes his articles. Alan is completely committed to the Highland way of life. He admires the Gaels, and identifies with their traditions as closely as any incomer possibly can, comparing their understanding of their environment with that of the American Indian. Their intimate knowledge and awareness of their topography is illustrated by their place names, and Alan gave a few examples. Bidean nam Bian (the highest mountain in Argyll), means Peak of the Hides, and is so named because, at some time, skins have been found there, possibly of deer which had starved, or been avalanched; or it may simply have been that the deer gathered there. The famous 'three sisters' of Glencoe, which the walker going down the glen will see on the left, are Beinn Fhada, which is the Long Hill, Gearr Aonach, the Short Ridge, and the Aonach Dhubh, the Black Ridge. Perfectly described, too, are the Aonach Eagach – the notched or toothed ridge, and the best-known landmark in the glen, the Bauchaille Etive Mor – the Big Shepherd of Etive. Glen Etive is on the other side of the mountain. Alan Thompson was intrigued by the fact that whereas deer often featured in Gaelic place names, such as Beinn Bhuiridh – the Mountain of the Roaring Stags – sheep were never mentioned. This was because the sheep came much later than the naming of the mountains, and at a time when the Gaelic language itself was proscribed by law.

Alan's attitude to the West Highland Way was, like many of his peers, rather ambivalent. As a lifelong outdoor man with a deep appreciation of the Scottish countryside, he sympathised with people's desire and need to enjoy those amenities, but was genuinely worried about the possible environmental consequences. He accepted my point that not everyone was a tiger on the mountain, and that for many people, schemes like the West Highland Way provided the only easy and safe access to the outdoors. He was puzzled, however, by what he saw as a contradiction in the Countryside Commission for Scotland's endorsement of the Way, while opposing expansion of skiing in the Cairngorms into the Western Corries, on the grounds of possible environmental damage. Another anomaly is that the Glencoe area first came into the ownership of the National Trust for Scotland largely through the efforts of a past president of the Scottish Mountaineering Club, P. J. H. Unna. Unna bequeathed his personal fortune to the Trust on the understanding that the area should be maintained as wilderness. Over the years, a great deal of effort has gone into the removal of intrusive signposts and markers, and many of Alan Thompson's colleagues feel that this work has now been nullified and the process reversed.

The plantation at Altnafeadh marks the beginning of a rocky scramble which takes you high above the floor of the glen, allowing a backward look along the route, and wonderful views of the peaks and ridges ahead. In certain conditions, the whole Glencoe and Rannoch area can be downright spooky, and it's not at all surprising that weird stories proliferate. A man who lived near here owned an old rocking-chair and, after the death of this man's brother in Glen Etive, the chair took to rocking by itself, in a rather unsettling manner. The rocking took place at odd moments, unaccountably and unpredictably. Many people saw the chair in motion, and theories were advanced—climatic changes causing contraction and expansion in the old wood, vibration, draughts and so on. Eventually, when the lady of the house had reached a state of nervous exhaustion, the old chair was taken out and burned. I could not find anyone who admitted to believing this story, but on the other hand, no one would state that it was definitely untrue. On the basis that tales like this add a little *frisson* to what can sometimes be a rather humdrum existence, I prefer to believe it.

The Glen of Weeping

The story of all stories in Glencoe is that of the massacre. By modern standards, it was a piffling affair, and an American soldier who was convicted of a much more full-blooded one in a recent war, had a statue raised in his honour. Remarkable then, that the outraged response to the Glencoe affair has reverberated through the Highlands for generations, and down to the present day. It was not the scale of the incident, or even any idea that the perpetrators were devils incarnate and the victims unsullied innocents, but rather the smell of treachery, and the betrayal of ancient Highland traditions of hospitality which colours the way people speak of the incident, even today.

The massacre of Glencoe took place in 1692, and was just one more incident in the subjugation, or pacification, as it was euphemistically known, of the Highlands. The Hanoverian King William III knew little of life in the Highlands and cared less; the people were looked on as savages who had to be brought to heel. The McDonalds were known to be staunchly Jacobite, and loyal to the Stuarts and King James VII. They also had a reputation as rumbustious trouble-makers, and were among the more notable of the clans which had

Old Glencoe road

taken arms against the Hanoverians. Hoping to speed up his 'Pacification' programme, King William had offered amnesty to all who took an oath of allegiance before the first of January 1692. McIain, Chief of the Glencoe McDonalds, after long deliberation, decided to sign. The journey from Glencoe to Invereray, where the document had to be witnessed, was a formidable one in those days, especially in January, and if we add to that the Chief's instinctive reluctance, combined with a natural Highland propensity for procrastination, it's not surprising that he was late. What is surprising is that he was only a day late, but the Sheriff Depute who had to take the oath was absent, and did not return until the fifth of January, when McDonald signed.

The then Secretary of State for Scotland, albeit to a foreign government, was Sir John Dalrymple, Master of Stair; a sworn enemy of all Jacobites, and of the McDonalds in particular. Ignoring the fact that several other eminent Chiefs had failed to sign the oath, Dalrymple decided to put paid to the McDonalds once and for all, and took advantage of an instruction from the King to 'Extirpate that sept of thieves'.

On the first of February, Captain Robert Campbell of Glenlyon (who had a personal grudge against the McDonalds), led a company into Glencoe on the pretext of a military exercise. For two weeks, the soldiers lived with the McDonalds as guests and friends, sharing their homes, food and drink. The sordid and bloody affair began about four o'clock in the morning, when the old Chief, McIain, was roused from his bed and shot in the back as he was pulling on his breeks. His wife, who witnessed the slaughter, was shamefully treated, and in the cold dark of the morning, men, women and children were rudely awakened to be shot, or hacked to death. The number of people killed is estimated at thirty-eight, but it is not known how many of those who made an escape into the bitter Highland winter also died. The operation was, in fact, a dismal failure. The object of wiping out the Glencoe McDonalds was not accomplished. The back-up troops which had been sent to seal off the escape routes from the glen, ran into bad weather, and were too late, and it is believed that some of the soldiers, appalled by what they were being commanded to do, connived at the escape of some of their intended victims.

There was a huge outcry in the country, but the outcome was predictable and familiar. An enquiry was set up, noises were made, and although no statue was erected to Dalrymple, he was exonerated by King William of charges of over-zealousness and barbarity, and granted a pension. Glencoe was a savage and sorry business, and there is no doubt that the political situation was exploited in the resolution of ancient enmities, and the settling of old scores between the Campbells and the McDonalds.

The Campbells are still known in Scotland, if jokingly, as the Black Campbells, and there is an inn in Glencoe which used to bear a sign over the door which said 'No dogs or Campbells'. The rivalry between the two names McDonald and Campbell survives now as a joke, but it's said that when the inn at one time came into the hands of a more tolerant landlord, the sign had to be re-painted. He did allow dogs.

There are many such stories, and my own favourite concerns an ancient Campbell, and an even more ancient McDonald who had been lifelong friends and drinking companions. Emerging one night from their favourite watering hole, considerably refreshed, McDonald, with no warning, landed a hefty oncer on his companion's earhole. Climbing groggily to his feet, old Campbell asked, 'What was that for?'

'For the massacre of Glencoe' said the pugilistic McDonald.

'Och, that was years ago!'

'Aye', growled McDonald, 'but I only heard about it in the pub tonight.'

Glencoe from the Devil's Staircase

The Devil's Staircase and the Head of the Lake of Grey Water

Some walkers will wish to pause at Glencoe village, which has varied accommodation – a visitors' centre, a good youth hostel, and the famous Clachaig Inn, which has been a popular meeting place for travellers and outdoor people since it was built in 1839. For those who wish to push on for Kinlochleven, the way is by Altnafeadh and the Devil's Staircase. Altnafeadh is another of the old cattle-drover's stances, and although the track is very obvious, it is marked by a sign which says 'Public footpath to Kinlochleven'. You are now facing a steep plod on a winding path which is very rocky and broken; though, when one considers that it was built around 1750 by the English army, it's remarkable that it is still usable at all. I sweated my way up here on a blistering June day, but the view from the summit cairn made it well worthwhile, and it was especially satisfying to look back over the rugged country already covered, with the barely visible, winding thread of the old military road snaking away to the Black Mount and Loch Tulla.

From your lofty vantage point, it's wonderful to look across at the craggy faces of the two Buachailles, and further along the glen, the three sisters of Glencoe – Beinn Fhada, Gearr Aonoch and Aonoch Dhubh. From this height, the towering peaks of Bidean nam Bian can be seen beyond the three sisters, whilst ahead, the track winds its way to Kinlochleven, and into the backdrop of the Mamore mountains, dominated by the huge bulk of Ben Nevis. From Loch Tulla onwards I had been keeping watch for an eagle, and it was on the descending stretch from the cairn on the Devil's Staircase that I finally saw one, sailing very high away over Glen Etive, on the far side of the Bauchaille Etive Mor. In spite of the great height and distance, it was unmistakably an eagle. People who live in the Highlands are quite used to excited tourists who have just seen an eagle, and don't usually bother to explain that what they were looking at was a buzzard. In fact, Scottish outdoor folk have nicknamed the buzzard the 'Englishman's Eagle'. On one occasion however, the tourists were correct, for a young, but fully-grown, eagle took to perching on posts in Glencoe, only yards from the main road, becoming probably the most photographed eagle in Scotland. This proved to be one of a number of young sea eagles released on the islands, as part of a re-stocking project. Once seen, it is very unlikely that the eagle will again be confused with anything else. It is vastly bigger than a buzzard, the wings much longer in proportion, stretching to a seven-foot span, and with a distinctly sharp angle to the leading edge. In silhouette, the tail and head are longer and slimmer than in the buzzard, and it is usually seen sailing and wheeling at tremendous heights.

It's all downhill from here to Kinlochleven, and though the walk traverses a lot of wild, unsheltered moorland, you are soon among thick woods, mainly of birch. Kinlochleven and the loch are hidden from view until one is almost upon them, but the cone-shaped peak of Beinn na Caillach can be seen beyond the Lairig Mhor, which is your next ascent. The main landmarks on this section are the Black-waterfoot dam, over to the right, and the six huge parallel pipes which carry the water down to Kinlochleven and the aluminium works. I thoroughly enjoyed this part of the West Highland Way, and not only because it was mostly downhill. The walking was good, and it was just before Kinlochleven came suddenly into view that a peregrine falcon shot from a rock just above my left ear, and went rocketing across the glen on some urgent business, ignoring the scrambling, undignified panic of several hoodie crows in its path.

Devil's Staircase to Kinlochleven

Loch Leven

In the Gaelic, Kinlochleven is Ceann Loch Lia Abhain – Head of the Lake of Grey Water. Loch Leven was bridged at Ballachulish in 1975, and before that, the road to Fort William and the north was connected by the Ballachulish ferry. Many a time, on concert tours, I had to make the agonising choice between a long delay in the queue for the ferry, and the drive on the switchback road around the loch. Even worse, was arriving after a dash through Glencoe or round from Oban, to see the ferrymen tying up for the day, and heading for the bar of the Ballachulish Hotel.

Before the construction of the Blackwaterfoot Dam, Kinlochleven consisted of two shooting lodges and a farm, but the aluminium smelting works transformed it into the first industrial town in the Highlands. In 1919 the *Oban Times* gave a description of Kinlochleven under the heading 'The Electric City of Kinlochleven'.

Kinlochleven is modern in every respect with a population of about 1400. It is well-planned and laid out. The streets are wide with an excellent surface. The houses are built on the terrace system. The village has a town hall, public school, recreation ground, bowling green, phone system, four churches, police station, fire station, barracks for single men, and a hostel for women. The town at night is a brilliant display of light. If, on a dark night one crosses the river to Invernesshire, one gets a most wonderful view of the town, glittering with lights from end to end. The scene is intensified by the dark background of a hill which rises immediately behind the town. Kinlochleven is therefore obviously unique in many respects as contrasted with any town in the UK.

Kinlochleven from the Lairig Mhor

Happy Hunting-grounds

At Kinlochleven, I spoke to four Dutch girls whom I had last seen at Inverarnan. They were students of landscape gardening, and were bright and observant people, and I asked them for their general impressions of the West Highland Way, and of Scotland. I was struck by the fact that all four had been astonished by the desolation on the Highland parts of the route, and by the great areas devoid of population in such a small country. I pointed out that this had not always been so. Many of these wilderness areas once supported healthy communities, and crops grew where there is now barren moor. The east shore of Loch Lomond, for example, was dotted along its length with little clachans,* where the people survived by fishing and growing crops, and where they made charcoal and smelted iron. We have already spoken of the great numbers of Highland cattle and sheep which were taken on the hoof to the markets of the lowlands and England, and even the seemingly sterile Lairig Mhor once provided summer grazing for the little black cattle; the women and children who cared for the beasts, coming up to spend the season in the shielings.*

I learned a little more about the use of the land in Scotland, when I went to Stronmilchan, near Dalmally, to talk to Willie Orr. Willie spent two years with the Forestry Commission, then worked as a hill shepherd for thirteen years. He then went to Stirling University, where he took a degree in economics and Scottish history, following this with a post-graduate course in Scottish land use in the nineteenth century.

I asked Willie if he thought that the nineteenth century uses and abuses of Scottish land still affected us today. He felt that this was so, and believed that the root causes of most of the problems lay in the ownership of land. The first great change had come with the infamous Highland clearances, when the people had been moved to make way for sheep. The well-being and needs of the ordinary people were totally ignored, the requirements of the landlords taking precedence. Willie demonstrated that this had continued to be the case until the present day, although there had been some dramatic changes.

The decline of sheep farming in the face of overseas competitions, coincided with a tremendous increase of wealth in the south. These were the two factors which gave rise to the deer forests, as the wealthy

* *clachan*: a small village or settlement   *shieling*: hut or temporary shelter

began to buy up Scottish land for recreational purposes. By the year 1906, no less than three million acres had been given over entirely to sport, meaning that this vast area was completely cleared of cattle and sheep. Benefit to local communities was minimal, the deer forests providing even less employment than had the sheep; so that the depopulation of the Highlands which had begun with the sheep, continued and was exacerbated by the expansion of the deer forests. Once again, the basic requirements of whole communities were sacrificed to indulge the wealthy few.

Willie Orr pointed out that not only the private landlords were culpable. Government management proved equally unsatisfactory. Towards the end of the First World War, the decision to plant huge tracts of land with sitka spruce was taken with the interests of the state in mind, not those of the native population. The planned development of forestry was never carried out in a way that would provide maximum employment, and keep as many people as possible in the Highlands, so that state ownership too failed the people.

Willie's conclusion was that sheep, deer and forestry had brought benefit to the few, and great deprivation to many. I asked him if things had improved, and received an emphatic 'No'. There were new problems: institutional or syndicate buying of land, and increasing ownership by foreigners, many of whom remained anonymous, and had no understanding of, or concern for, the local population. The nationality of an owner, however, was less important than his attitude. An uncaring Scottish landlord could be as destructive as anyone else. There are, of course, responsible landlords, and well-run estates, but there is no more to stop an owner clearing thousands of acres now, than there was a hundred years ago.

Despite all this, Willie Orr feels that there is some cause for optimism, especially in the increasing awareness of young Highlanders of their problems and how they can be tackled. What is required is proper land registry, so that it is known who owns what, and secondly, an overall plan which would integrate the interests of agriculture, sport, forestry and tourism. The alternative is that the Highlands of Scotland could quickly become, once again, what Willie calls 'The Happy Hunting Ground of the Rich'.

Mo Mhollachd aig na Caoraich Mhor

My curses on the Cheviot yowe!*
Where are all my kinfolk now?
Fled their homes so long ago,
When I was still a laddie.

Sixty years and three have gone,
And silent is the but and ben;*
Sheep are here where once were men,
And Sutherland deserted.

Patrick Sellar, roast in hell,
With the ones you served so well;
The flames that tolled the crofters' knell,
I hope you've had your fill o'.

Duchess-Countess, skin like milk,
Where now are your gowns of silk?
To the grave with all your ilk,*
You couldn't take them wi' you.

All my curses on the scum,
Who sent my clansmen o'er the foam;
Scattered far, without a home,
Nor food, nor heat, nor shelter.

My curses on the Cheviot yowe,
Where are all my kinsfolk now?
Fled their country long ago,
And left behind, a desert.

* *Yowe*: ewe   *But and Ben*: a two-roomed house   *ilk*: kind

The title of this song means 'My curses on the big sheep', and the translation from the Gaelic was made by Willie Morrison, who was brought up on a croft in Durness, where his father still lives. The croft borders on the area which was known as the 'Ceannabeine Clearances'. The Duchess-Countess was the Duchess of Sutherland, a Countess in her own right, and the wife of the Duke of Sutherland. The family carried out some of the most extensive and rigorous clearances in Scotland, and one of their factors, Patrick Sellar, raised himself from obscurity to notoriety by the enthusiasm with which he carried out evictions on behalf of his masters. So ready with the torch was he, that he became known as the 'Fire Raiser'.

Kinlochleven makes a good stopping place before the last leg of the West Highland Way. There is good accommodation, friendly people, and some fine walks. I contented myself with a snack in the Shieling Café, and walked round the head of the loch to the other side of the town, where a cast-iron sign on a post says: 'Public footpath to Fort William by the Lairig'.

The Way on the Lairig Mhor to Fort William section

Children of the Dead End and the Great High Pass

The track up to the Lairig Mhor is another steep and rocky one which, after a mile or so, joins Caulfield's military road. This is a clearly defined track in good condition, but the exposure is almost total on the long haul to Fort William, and in bad weather this stretch can present a dreich* prospect. Ahead of you and to your left, is the towering cone of Beinn na Caillach – the Old Woman's Mountain, and on the other side of the narrow, serpentine waters of Loch Leven, the Pap of Glencoe. Looking back, you can trace your long descent from the Devil's Staircase, Kinlochleven lies below you like a toy town, and the great water pipes run down the hill from the Blackwaterfoot dam. The building of this dam in the early 1900s was one of the very last projects of its kind in this country to be undertaken by sheer muscle power. It was constructed by itinerant navvies, mainly Irish and Scots, and many of them travelled great distances on foot to find work here.

On Lairig Mhor

* *dreich*: dull, dreary

There's a poem by Patrick McGill, which begins:

Though up may be up, and down my be down,
Life will make everything even;
And the man who starves in Greenock town
Will fatten in Kinlochleven.

They 'fattened' on sixpence an hour, and as much overtime as they could physically survive. In a wonderful book called *Children of the Dead End*, Patrick McGill describes the lives of these people, and the dreadful conditions under which they lived and worked. Accidents were common, and sometimes quite horrific. McGill describes a man striking a concealed detonator, and having a pick-head driven through his throat by the explosion; another hanging, trapped by the legs, forty feet up in the scaffolding, was taken down raving and hysterical. There was much drunkenness and brawling, and many deaths occurred when men set off to walk to Kingshouse for a night of drinking. Many were lost, and succumbed to the weather on the return journey, their bodies often unrecovered until the spring thaws. To be paid off at the Blackwaterfoot dam in winter could be a virtual death sentence, as walking to another job was nearly impossible. Patrick McGill's characters now live only in his books. People like Hell-Fire Gaghey, Ben the Moocher, Moleskin Joe, Blasting Mick, and Carroty Dan. Some lie in the little cemetery in the hills, near the dam itself. There are twenty stones there, and one is marked simply, 'Unknown'. Here lie the remains of a man who died of exposure on his way to find work, and who now rests in what must be one of the loneliest graveyards in the world.

The Lairig Mhor was the most desolate part of my walk so far. I did not see another human being from beginning to end. There were a few sheep, and at one point a pair of ravens tumbled over my head. Even at this time of year, the high glen had a barren aspect, and I was grateful for the snatches of sunshine which dried me out between showers. There were signs of past human activity, however, in the deserted Tigh na Sleubhaich – the House of the Hill of the Gullies, and the ruins at Blar a Chaorainn – field of the rowan. About half-way to Fort William you will see, lying down to your left, the waters of Loch Lunn Da Bhra – in English, Lundavra – and a little further on, the Way parts company with the military road, to cross over into Glen Nevis. The weary walker may prefer to follow the road down into Fort William, and indeed, this route is very attractive, but there is no

Above Approaching Glen Nevis *Below* Glen Nevis Youth Hostel

doubt that in good weather, the Glen Nevis section is spectacular. Having now left almost a hundred rough miles behind, ending with the high desolation of the Lairig Mhor, the sudden appearance of the suburbs of Fort William comes as something of an anticlimax. As I shouldered my way through the crowds of tourists, attracting not even a glance, I could not help asking myself, 'What's wrong? Don't they know I've just walked in? I'm really here. I did it!' Fort William seemed unimpressed.

Fort William

Envoi

As I strode down towards the suburbs of Fort William, I noticed a lad walking purposefully towards me on the other side of the road. He was a hardy-looking character in rought outdoor gear, with well-worn boots, and a small rucksack on his back. As I caught his eye, I nodded and greeted him in that bluff comradely way we outdoor men have. 'Heading for Kinlochleven?' I asked. 'Och no,' was the reply. 'I'm just taking these frozen chickens up to my Auntie Jeannie.'

Addresses

Friends of Loch Lomond
Mrs Hannah Barr-Stirling
Auchendarroch
Tarbet
Dunbartonshire, G83 7DQ

Plant a Pine Scheme
Keith Graham
Arnclerich Cottage
Port of Menteith
Central Scotland

Note: The climbers' huts marked on the map (apart from the Rowchoish bothy) are open only to members of mountaineering clubs. Bookings should be made through the applicant's club; the name and address of the hut custodian can be obtained from the Mountaineering Council of Scotland.

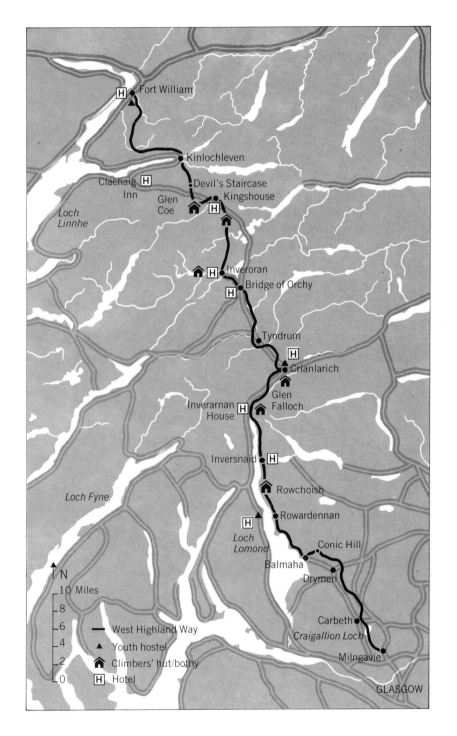

Fort William

Kinlochleven

Clachaig Inn

Devil's Staircase

Glen Coe

Kingshouse

Loch Linnhe

Inveroran

Bridge of Orchy

Tyndrum

Crianlarich

Glen Falloch

Inverarnan House

Inversnaid

Loch Fyne

Rowchoish

Rowardennan

Loch Lomond

Conic Hill

Balmaha

Drymen

Carbeth

Craigallion Loch

Milngavie

GLASGOW

↑ N

10 Miles
8
6
4
2
0

— West Highland Way
▲ Youth hostel
⌂ Climbers' hut/bothy
H Hotel